Conventions and Recommendations of
Unesco concerning the protection of
the cultural heritage

Conventions and Recommendations of Unesco concerning the protection of the cultural heritage

Unesco

4140

P (UNE)

First published in 1983 by the United Nations
Educational, Scientific and Cultural Organization
7 place de Fontenoy, 75700 Paris
Printed by Imprimeries Populaires, Geneva

Reprinted and updated 1985

ISBN 92-3-102101-X
French edition: 92-3-202101-3

Printed in Switzerland

Contents

—

Introduction

The preservation of the world's cultural heritage is one of the essential functions laid on the Organization by its Constitution. It calls for the adoption of appropriate legislation defining the nature and scope of the protection to be provided, specifying the property involved and setting out the measures which will afford such protection. Of comparatively recent date, this legislation is being built up gradually. It is to be found at two distinct levels—the international and the national.

Internationally, there is a series of conventions and recommendations adopted by Unesco or under its auspices which lay down the rules that should govern the safeguarding of the heritage. Since this heritage concerns the minds of men and is the fruit and the bearer of their culture, it must be protected against the very varied dangers threatening it, wherever its component parts may be and to whatever civilization they belong.

Some of these conventions and recommendations are more directly concerned with international relations and lay down the rules that States are expected to observe in their relations with each other, whether at war or peace. Such are Unesco's instruments on the protection of the cultural heritage in the event of armed conflict, on the prohibition of the import of cultural property against the will of the State on whose territory it was originally located, on international assistance for the protection of the world cultural and natural heritage, and on international co-operation with regard to archaeological excavations.

Unesco's normative action is nevertheless not confined to inter-State relations. The Organization has also defined the principles and standards that should govern the protection of the cultural heritage at the national level, and has listed the measures to be taken by every State to safeguard the cultural property on its own territory. This has been done mainly by means of recommendations to Member States which, under the Rules of Procedure concerning Recommendations to Member States and International Conventions covered by the terms of Article IV, paragraph 4, of the Constitution are instruments in which 'the General Conference formulates principles and norms for the international regulation of any particular question and invites Member States to take whatever legislative or other steps may be required—in conformity with the constitutional practice of each State and the nature of the question under consideration—to apply the principles and norms aforesaid within their respective territories' (Article 1 (b)). These are therefore norms which are not subject to ratification but which Member States are invited to apply. Emanating from the Organization's supreme governing body and hence possessing great authority, recommendations are intended to influence the development of national laws and practices.

When they are adopted by the General Conference, international conventions as well as recommendations to Member States are drafted in accordance with the above-mentioned rules of procedure which provide for the following stages. First a preliminary study is made of the technical and legal aspects of the question to be regulated at the international level. This study must be submitted for prior consideration to the Executive Board, whose responsibility it is to include the proposal for international regulation in the agenda of the General Conference. The General Conference is then required to decide on the desirability of the regulation contemplated and on the form which such a regulation should take (convention or recommendation). The Director-General is then instructed to prepare a preliminary report setting forth the position with regard to the problem to be regulated and to the possible scope of the regulating action proposed.

Member States are invited to present their comments and observations on this report. In the light of these comments and observations, the Director-General prepares a final report containing one or more drafts of the convention or recommendation, which he communicates to Member States. This final report is submitted either direct to the General Conference or, if the Conference has so decided, to a special committee of governmental experts. The General Conference considers the draft texts submitted to it and, if it sees fit, adopts the instrument.

Recommendations are adopted by a simple majority whereas a two-thirds majority is required for the adoption of conventions.

The conventions and recommendations adopted by Unesco for the protection of cultural property are listed below in chronological order:
1. Convention for the Protection of Cultural Property in the Event of Armed Conflict, with Regulations for the Execution of the Convention (Intergovernmental Conference, The Hague, 14 May 1954).

2. Protocol for the Protection of Cultural Property in the Event of Armed Conflict (Intergovernmental Conference, The Hague, 14 May 1954).
3. Recommendation on International Principles Applicable to Archaeological Excavations (General Conference, New Delhi, 5 December 1956).
4. Recommendation concerning the Most Effective Means of Rendering Museums Accessible to Everyone (General Conference, Paris, 14 December 1960).
5. Recommendation concerning the Safeguarding of the Beauty and Character of Landscapes and Sites (General Conference, Paris, 11 December 1962).
6. Recommendation on the Means of Prohibiting and Preventing the Illicit Export, Import and Transfer of Ownership of Cultural Property (General Conference, Paris, 19 November 1964).
7. Recommendation concerning the Preservation of Cultural Property Endangered by Public or Private works (General Conference, Paris, 19 November 1968).
8. Convention on the Means of Prohibiting and Preventing the Illicit Import, Export and Transfer of Ownership of Cultural Property (General Conference, Paris, 14 November 1970).
9. Convention concerning the Protection of the World Cultural and Natural Heritage (General Conference, Paris, 16 November 1972).
10. Recommendation concerning the Protection, at National Level, of the Cultural and Natural Heritage (General Conference, Paris, 16 November 1972).
11. Recommendation concerning the International Exchange of Cultural Property (General Conference, Nairobi, 26 November 1976).
12. Recommendation concerning the Safeguarding and Contemporary Role of Historic Areas (General Conference, Nairobi, 26 November 1976).
13. Recommendation for the Protection of Movable Cultural Property (General Conference, Paris, 28 November 1978).
14. Recommendation for the Safeguarding and Preservation of Moving Images (General Conference, Belgrade, 27 October 1980).

Although the recommendations of the General Conference are not subject to ratification, the mere fact that they have been adopted entails obligations even for those Member States that neither voted for it nor approved it. The same is true of international conventions adopted by the General Conference, in the case of Member States which have not ratified them, or do not intend to do so. This is the implication of Article VIII of the Constitution, while Article IV, paragraph 4, quoted above, provides that 'each of the Member States shall submit recommendations or conventions to its competent authorities within a period of one year from the close of the session of the General Conference at which they were adopted'. In this connection, the General Conference stated at its twelfth session that:

the General Conference also feels bound to draw attention once again to the distinction to be drawn between the obligation to submit an instrument to the competent authorities, on the one hand, and the ratification of a convention or the acceptance of a recommendation, on the other. Their submission to the competent authorities does not imply that conventions should necessarily be ratified or that recommendations should be accepted in their entirety. On the other hand, it is incumbent on Member States to submit *all* recommendations and conventions *without exception* to the competent authorities, even if measures of ratification or acceptance are not contemplated in a particular case.

The above-mentioned Rules of Procedure concerning recommendations and conventions also contain, in Chapter VI regarding the procedure for submission and examination of reports, the following provisions:

Article 16
1. Member States shall submit to the General Conference special reports on the action they have taken to give effect to conventions or recommendations adopted by the General Conference.
2. Initial reports relating to any convention or recommendation adopted shall be transmitted not less than two months prior to the first ordinary session of the General Conference following that at which such recommendation or convention was adopted.
3. The General Conference may further request Member States to submit, by prescribed dates, additional reports giving such further information as may be necessary.

Article 17
At the first ordinary session following that at which a convention or recommendation has been adopted, and at any subsequent session, if it so decides, the General Conference shall consider the special reports submitted by Member States in connexion with the convention or recommendation in question.

Article 18
The General Conference shall embody its comments on the action taken by Member States in pursuance of a convention or recommendation in one or more general reports, which the Conference shall prepare at such times as it may deem appropriate.[1]

Article 19
The General Conference's reports on the action taken by Member States in pursuance of a convention or recommendation shall be transmitted to Member States, to the United Nations, to National Commissions, and to any other authorities specified by the General Conference.

The texts published in this collection are classified by type of instrument: A. Conventions, B. Recommendations, and are reproduced in chronological order.

---

1. These reports are published in Volume 1 of the *Records of the General Conference (Resolutions)*.

A. Conventions

Convention for the Protection of Cultural Property in the Event of Armed Conflict (the 'Hague Convention'), with Regulations for the Execution of the Convention, as well as the Protocol to the Convention and the Conference Resolution[1]

Introduction

This Convention is a sequel to the fourth Convention of 1907 concerning the laws and customs of warfare on land, which instituted for the first time a rudimentary form of international protection for edifices devoted to the arts and sciences and for historical monuments. It contains provisions for the safeguarding of movable or immovable property of great importance to the cultural heritage of peoples, irrespective of its origin or ownership, and makes respect for such property obligatory.

The safeguarding of such property implies that the States within whose territory it is situated will take all necessary protective measures in time of peace.

Respect for protected property is an obligation both on the territorial State and on its enemies in time of armed conflict. Such respect for protected property implies that the parties to the Convention refrain from any use of it which might lay it open to destruction and from any act of hostility directed against it. They further undertake to prohibit and, if necessary prevent any form of theft, pillage, misappropriation or vandalism directed against cultural property.

Provision is made for special protection for cultural property of very great importance and for the refuges intended to shelter it.

The procedures for application of the Convention are set out in regulations for its execution which, on the initiative of the Director-General of Unesco, were implemented for the first time during the 1967 Middle East conflict.

The Convention also provides that the Contracting Parties shall, at least once

---

1. Adopted at The Hague, on 14 May 1954, by an International Conference of States convened by Unesco.

IV.A.3.Intro.1

every four years, forward to the Director-General of Unesco a report on any measures being taken, prepared or contemplated in fulfilment of the Convention and of the Regulations for its execution.

The Convention came into force on 7 August 1956.

The Protocol adopted by the Conference which met at The Hague at the same time as the Convention of 1954 was adopted forbids the Contracting States to export cultural property from territories under their occupation. Furthermore, those States must take all necessary steps to prevent such exportation by anyone.

If, despite these steps, an item of cultural property is exported from an occupied territory, it must be returned to the competent authorities of that territory upon the cessation of hostilities, it being understood that any indemnities due to purchasers or holders in good faith will be paid by the previously occupying State. The Protocol stipulates that cultural property transferred from an occupied territory shall never be retained as war reparations.

The Protocol came into force on 7 August 1956.

United Nations Educational, Scientific and
Cultural Organization

Convention for the Protection
of Cultural Property in the Event
# of Armed Conflict

Adopted at The Hague, 14 May 1954

The High Contracting Parties,

Recognizing that cultural property has suffered grave damage during recent armed conflicts and that, by reason of the developments in the technique of warfare, it is in increasing danger of destruction;

Being convinced that damage to cultural property belonging to any people whatsoever means damage to the cultural heritage of all mankind, since each people makes its contribution to the culture of the world;

Considering that the preservation of the cultural heritage is of great importance for all peoples of the world and that it is important that this heritage should receive international protection;

Guided by the principles concerning the protection of cultural property during armed conflict, as established in the Conventions of The Hague of 1899 and of 1907 and in the Washington Pact of 15 April, 1935;

Being of the opinion that such protection cannot be effective unless both national and international measures have been taken to organize it in time of peace;

Being determined to take all possible steps to protect cultural property;

Have agreed upon the following provisions:

IV.A.3

Chapter I. General provisions regarding protection

Article 1. Definition of cultural property

For the purposes of the present Convention, the term 'cultural property' shall cover, irrespective of origin or ownership:

(a) movable or immovable property of great importance to the cultural heritage of every people, such as monuments of architecture, art or history, whether religious or secular; archaeological sites; groups of buildings which, as a whole, are of historical or artistic interest; works of art; manuscripts, books and other objects of artistic, historical or archaeological interest; as well as scientific collections and important collections of books or archives or of reproductions of the property defined above;

(b) buildings whose main and effective purpose is to preserve or exhibit the movable cultural property defined in sub-paragraph (a) such as museums, large libraries and depositories of archives, and refuges intended to shelter, in the event of armed conflict, the movable cultural property defined in sub-paragraph (a);

(c) centres containing a large amount of cultural property as defined in sub-paragraphs (a) and (b), to be known as 'centres containing monuments'.

Article 2. Protection of cultural property

For the purposes of the present Convention, the protection of cultural property shall comprise the safeguarding of and respect for such property.

Article 3. Safeguarding of cultural property

The High Contracting Parties undertake to prepare in time of peace for the safeguarding of cultural property situated within their own territory against the foreseeable effects of an armed conflict, by taking such measures as they consider appropriate.

Article 4. Respect for cultural property

1. The High Contracting Parties undertake to respect cultural property situated within their own territory as well as within the territory of other High Contracting Parties by refraining from any use of the property and its immediate surroundings or of the appliances in use for its protection for purposes which are likely to expose it to destruction or damage in the event of armed

conflict; and by refraining from any act of hostility directed against such property.

2. The obligations mentioned in paragraph 1 of the present Article may be waived only in cases where military necessity imperatively requires such a waiver.

3. The High Contracting Parties further undertake to prohibit, prevent and, if necessary, put a stop to any form of theft, pillage or misappropriation of, and any acts of vandalism directed against, cultural property. They shall refrain from requisitioning movable cultural property situated in the territory of another High Contracting Party.

4. They shall refrain from any act directed by way of reprisals against cultural property.

5. No High Contracting Party may evade the obligations incumbent upon it under the present Article, in respect of another High Contracting Party, by reason of the fact that the latter has not applied the measures of safeguard referred to in Article 3.

Article 5. Occupation

1. Any High Contracting Party in occupation of the whole or part of the territory of another High Contracting Party shall as far as possible support the competent national authorities of the occupied country in safeguarding and preserving its cultural property.

2. Should it prove necessary to take measures to preserve cultural property situated in occupied territory and damaged by military operations, and should the competent national authorities be unable to take such measures, the Occupying Power shall, as far as possible, and in close co-operation with such authorities, take the most necessary measures of preservation.

3. Any High Contracting Party whose government is considered their legitimate government by members of a resistance movement, shall, if possible, draw their attention to the obligation to comply with those provisions of the Convention dealing with respect for cultural property.

Article 6. Distinctive marking of cultural property

In accordance with the provisions of Article 16, cultural property may bear a distinctive emblem so as to facilitate its recognition.

Article 7. Military measures

1. The High Contracting Parties undertake to introduce in time of peace into their military regulations or instructions such provisions as may ensure observance of the present Convention, and to foster in the members of their armed forces a spirit of respect for the culture and cultural property of all peoples.

2. The High Contracting Parties undertake to plan or establish in peace-time, within their armed forces, services or specialist personnel whose purpose will be to secure respect for cultural property and to co-operate with the civilian authorities responsible for safeguarding it.

Chapter II. Special protection

Article 8. Granting of special protection

1. There may be placed under special protection a limited number of refuges intended to shelter movable cultural property in the event of armed conflict, of centres containing monuments and other immovable cultural property of very great importance, provided that they:
(a) are situated at an adequate distance from any large industrial centre or from any important military objective constituting a vulnerable point, such as, for example, an aerodrome, broadcasting station, establishment engaged upon work of national defence, a port or railway station of relative importance or a main line of communication;
(b) are not used for military purposes.

2. A refuge for movable cultural property may also be placed under special protection, whatever its location, if it is so constructed that, in all probability, it will not be damaged by bombs.

3. A centre containing monuments shall be deemed to be used for military purposes whenever it is used for the movement of military personnel or material, even in transit. The same shall apply whenever activities directly connected with military operations, the stationing of military personnel, or the production of war material are carried on within the centre.

4. The guarding of cultural property mentioned in paragraph 1 above by armed custodians specially empowered to do so, or the presence, in the vicinity of such cultural property, of police forces normally responsible for the maintenance of public order shall not be deemed to be used for military purposes.

5. If any cultural property mentioned in paragraph 1 of the present Article is situated near an important military objective as defined in the said paragraph, it may nevertheless be placed under special protection if the High Contracting Party asking for that protection undertakes, in the event of armed conflict, to make no use of the objective and particularly, in the case of a port, railway station or aerodrome, to divert all traffic therefrom. In that event, such diversion shall be prepared in time of peace.

6. Special protection is granted to cultural property by its entry in the 'International Register of Cultural Property under Special Protection'. This entry shall only be made, in accordance with the provisions of the present Convention and under the conditions provided for in the Regulations for the execution of the Convention.

Article 9. Immunity of cultural property under special protection

The High Contracting Parties undertake to ensure the immunity of cultural property under special protection by refraining, from the time of entry in the International Register, from any act of hostility directed against such property and, except for the cases provided for in paragraph 5 of Article 8, from any use of such property or its surroundings for military purposes.

Article 10. Identification and control

During an armed conflict, cultural property under special protection shall be marked with the distinctive emblem described in Article 16, and shall be open to international control as provided for in the Regulations for the execution of the Convention.

Article 11. Withdrawal of immunity

1. If one of the High Contracting Parties commits, in respect of any item of cultural property under special protection, a violation of the obligations under Article 9, the opposing Party shall, so long as this violation persists, be released from the obligation to ensure the immunity of the property concerned. Nevertheless, whenever possible, the latter Party shall first request the cessation of such violation within a reasonable time.

2. Apart from the case provided for in paragraph 1 of the present Article, immunity shall be withdrawn from cultural property under special protection only in exceptional cases of unavoidable military necessity, and only for such time as that necessity continues. Such necessity can be established only by the

officer commanding a force the equivalent of a division in size or larger. Whenever circumstances permit, the opposing Party shall be notified, a reasonable time in advance, of the decision to withdraw immunity.

3. The Party withdrawing immunity shall, as soon as possible, so inform the Commissioner-General for cultural property provided for in the Regulations for the execution of the Convention, in writing, stating the reasons.

Chapter III. Transport of cultural property

Article 12. Transport under special protection

1. Transport exclusively engaged in the transfer of cultural property, whether within a territory or to another territory, may, at the request of the High Contracting Party concerned, take place under special protection in accordance with the conditions specified in the Regulations for the execution of the Convention.

2. Transport under special protection shall take place under the international supervision provided for in the aforesaid Regulations and shall display the distinctive emblem described in Article 16.

3. The High Contracting Parties shall refrain from any act of hostility directed against transport under special protection.

Article 13. Transport in urgent cases

1. If a High Contracting Party considers that the safety of certain cultural property requires its transfer and that the matter is of such urgency that the procedure laid down in Article 12 cannot be followed, especially at the beginning of an armed conflict, the transport may display the distinctive emblem described in Article 16, provided that an application for immunity referred to in Article 12 has not already been made and refused. As far as possible, notification of transfer should be made to the opposing Parties. Nevertheless, transport conveying cultural property to the territory of another country may not display the distinctive emblem unless immunity has been expressly granted to it.

2. The High Contracting Parties shall take, so far as possible, the necessary precautions to avoid acts of hostility directed against the transport described in paragraph 1 of the present Article and displaying the distinctive emblem.

Article 14. Immunity from seizure, capture and prize

1. Immunity from seizure, placing in prize, or capture shall be granted to:
(a) cultural property enjoying the protection provided for in Article 12 or that provided for in Article 13;
(b) the means of transport exclusively engaged in the transfer of such cultural property.

2. Nothing in the present Article shall limit the right of visit and search.

Chapter IV. Personnel

Article 15. Personnel

As far as is consistent with the interests of security, personnel engaged in the protection of cultural property shall, in the interests of such property, be respected and, if they fall into the hands of the opposing Party, shall be allowed to continue to carry out their duties whenever the cultural property for which they are responsible has also fallen into the hands of the opposing Party.

Chapter V. The distinctive emblem

Article 16. Emblem of the convention

1. The distinctive emblem of the Convention shall take the form of a shield, pointed below, per saltire blue and white (a shield consisting of a royal-blue square, one of the angles of which forms the point of the shield, and of a royal-blue triangle above the square, the space on either side being taken up by a white triangle).

2. The emblem shall be used alone, or repeated three times in a triangular formation (one shield below), under the conditions provided for in Article 17.

Article 17. Use of the emblem

1. The distinctive emblem repeated three times may be used only as a means of identification of:
(a) immovable cultural property under special protection;
(b) the transport of cultural property under the conditions provided for in Articles 12 and 13;
(c) improvised refuges, under the conditions provided for in the Regulations for the execution of the Convention.

IV.A.3

2. The distinctive emblem may be used alone only as a means of identification of:

(a) cultural property not under special protection;

(b) the persons responsible for the duties of control in accordance with the Regulations for the execution of the Convention;

(c) the personnel engaged in the protection of cultural property;

(d) the identity cards mentioned in the Regulations for the execution of the Convention.

3. During an armed conflict, the use of the distinctive emblem in any other cases than those mentioned in the preceding paragraphs of the present Article, and the use for any purpose whatever of a sign resembling the distinctive emblem, shall be forbidden.

4. The distinctive emblem may not be placed on any immovable cultural property unless at the same time there is displayed an authorization duly dated and signed by the competent authority of the High Contracting Party.

Chapter VI. Scope of application of the Convention

Article 18. Application of the Convention

1. Apart from the provisions which shall take effect in time of peace, the present Convention shall apply in the event of declared war or of any other armed conflict which may arise between two or more of the High Contracting Parties, even if the state of war is not recognized by one or more of them.

2. The Convention shall also apply to all cases of partial or total occupation of the territory of a High Contracting Party, even if the said occupation meets with no armed resistance.

3. If one of the Powers in conflict is not a Party to the present Convention, the Powers which are Parties thereto shall nevertheless remain bound by it in their mutual relations. They shall furthermore be bound by the Convention, in relation to the said Power, if the latter has declared that it accepts the provisions thereof and so long as it applies them.

Article 19. Conflicts not of an international character

1. In the event of an armed conflict not of an international character occurring within the territory of one of the High Contracting Parties, each party to

the conflict shall be bound to apply, as a minimum, the provisions of the present Convention which relate to respect for cultural property.

2. The parties to the conflict shall endeavour to bring into force, by means of special agreements, all or part of the other provisions of the present Convention.

3. The United Nations Educational, Scientific and Cultural Organization may offer its services to the parties to the conflict.

4. The application of the preceding provisions shall not affect the legal status of the parties to the conflict.

Chapter VII. Execution of the Convention

Article 20. Regulations for the execution of the Convention

The procedure by which the present Convention is to be applied is defined in the Regulations for its execution, which constitute an integral part thereof.

Article 21. Protecting powers

The present Convention and the Regulations for its execution shall be applied with the co-operation of the Protecting Powers responsible for safeguarding the interests of the Parties to the conflict.

Article 22. Conciliation procedure

1. The Protecting Powers shall lend their good offices in all cases where they may deem it useful in the interests of cultural property, particularly if there is disagreement between the Parties to the conflict as to the application or interpretation of the provisions of the present Convention or the Regulations for its execution.

2. For this purpose, each of the Protecting Powers may, either at the invitation of one Party, of the Director-General of the United Nations Educational, Scientific and Cultural Organization, or on its own initiative, propose to the Parties to the conflict a meeting of their representatives, and in particular of the authorities responsible for the protection of cultural property, if considered appropriate on suitably chosen neutral territory. The Parties to the conflict shall be bound to give effect to the proposals for meeting made to them.

The Protecting Powers shall propose for approval by the Parties to the conflict a person belonging to a neutral Power or a person presented by the Director-General of the United Nations Educational, Scientific and Cultural Organization, which person shall be invited to take part in such a meeting in the capacity of Chairman.

Article 23. Assistance of Unesco

1. The High Contracting Parties may call upon the United Nations Educational, Scientific and Cultural Organization for technical assistance in organizing the protection of their cultural property, or in connexion with any other problem arising out of the application of the present Convention or the Regulations for its execution. The Organization shall accord such assistance within the limits fixed by its programme and by its resources.

2. The Organization is authorized to make, on its own initiative, proposals on this matter to the High Contracting Parties.

Article 24. Special agreements

1. The High Contracting Parties may conclude special agreements for all matters concerning which they deem it suitable to make separate provision.

2. No special agreement may be concluded which would diminish the protection afforded by the present Convention to cultural property and to the personnel engaged in its protection.

Article 25. Dissemination of the Convention

The High Contracting Parties undertake, in time of peace as in time of armed conflict, to disseminate the text of the present Convention and the Regulations for its execution as widely as possible in their respective countries. They undertake, in particular, to include the study thereof in their programmes of military and, if possible, civilian training, so that its principles are made known to the whole population, especially the armed forces and personnel engaged in the protection of cultural property.

Article 26. Translations reports

1. The High Contracting Parties shall communicate to one another, through the Director-General of the United Nations Educational, Scientific and Cultural Organization, the official translations of the present Convention and of the Regulations for its execution.

IV.A.3

2. Furthermore, at least once every four years, they shall forward to the Director-General a report giving whatever information they think suitable concerning any measures being taken, prepared or contemplated by their respective administrations in fulfilment of the present Convention and of the Regulations for its execution.

Article 27. Meetings

1. The Director-General of the United Nations Educational, Scientific and Cultural Organization may, with the approval of the Executive Board, convene meetings of representatives of the High Contracting Parties. He must convene such a meeting if at least one-fifth of the High Contracting Parties so request.

2. Without prejudice to any other functions which have been conferred on it by the present Convention or the Regulations for its execution, the purpose of the meeting will be to study problems concerning the application of the Convention and of the Regulations for its execution, and to formulate recommendations in respect thereof.

3. The meeting may further undertake a revision of the Convention or the Regulations for its execution if the majority of the High Contracting Parties are represented, and in accordance with the provisions of Article 39.

Article 28. Sanctions

The High Contracting Parties undertake to take, within the framework of their ordinary criminal jurisdiction, all necessary steps to prosecute and impose penal or disciplinary sanctions upon those persons, of whatever nationality, who commit or order to be committed a breach of the present Convention.

Final provisions

Article 29. Languages

1. The present Convention is drawn up in English, French, Russian and Spanish, the four texts being equally authoritative.

2. The United Nations Educational, Scientific and Cultural Organization shall arrange for translations of the Convention into the other official languages of its General Conference.

IV.A.3

Article 30. Signature

The present Convention shall bear the date of 14 May, 1954 and, until the date of 31 December, 1954, shall remain open for signature by all States invited to the Conference which met at The Hague from 21 April, 1954 to 14 May, 1954.

Article 31. Ratification

1. The present Convention shall be subject to ratification by signatory States in accordance with their respective constitutional procedures.

2. The instruments of ratification shall be deposited with the Director-General of the United Nations Educational, Scientific and Cultural Organization.

Article 32. Accession

From the date of its entry into force, the present Convention shall be open for accession by all States mentioned in Article 30 which have not signed it, as well as any other State invited to accede by the Executive Board of the United Nations Educational, Scientific and Cultural Organization. Accession shall be effected by the deposit of an instrument of accession with the Director-General of the United Nations Educational, Scientific and Cultural Organization.

Article 33. Entry into force

1. The present Convention shall enter into force three months after five instruments of ratification have been deposited.

2. Thereafter, it shall enter into force, for each High Contracting Party, three months after the deposit of its instrument of ratification or accession.

3. The situations referred to in Articles 18 and 19 shall give immediate effect to ratifications or accessions deposited by the Parties to the conflict either before or after the beginning of hostilities or occupation. In such cases the Director-General of the United Nations Educational, Scientific and Cultural Organization shall transmit the communications referred to in Article 38 by the speediest method.

Article 34. Effective application

1. Each State Party to the Convention on the date of its entry into force shall take all necessary measures to ensure its effective application within a period of six months after such entry into force.

2. This period shall be six months from the date of deposit of the instruments of ratification or accession for any State which deposits its instrument of ratification or accession after the date of the entry into force of the Convention.

Article 35. Territorial extension of the Convention

Any High Contracting Party may, at the time of ratification or accession, or at any time thereafter, declare by notification addressed to the Director-General of the United Nations Educational, Scientific and Cultural Organization, that the present Convention shall extend to all or any of the territories for whose international relations it is responsible. The said notification shall take effect three months after the date of its receipt.

Article 36. Relation to previous conventions

1. In the relations between Powers which are bound by the Conventions of The Hague concerning the Laws and Customs of War on Land (IV) and concerning Naval Bombardment in Time of War (IX), whether those of 29 July, 1899 or those of 18 October, 1907, and which are Parties to the present Convention, this last Convention shall be supplementary to the aforementioned Convention (IX) and to the Regulations annexed to the aforementioned Convention (IV) and shall substitute for the emblem described in Article 5 of the aforementioned Convention (IX) the emblem described in Article 16 of the present Convention, in cases in which the present Convention and the Regulations for its execution provide for the use of this distinctive emblem.

2. In the relations between Powers which are bound by the Washington Pact of 15 April, 1935 for the Protection of Artistic and Scientific Institutions and of Historic Monuments (Roerich Pact) and which are Parties to the present Convention, the latter Convention shall be supplementary to the Roerich Pact and shall substitute for the distinguishing flag described in Article III of the Pact the emblem defined in Article 16 of the present Convention, in cases in which the present Convention and the Regulations for its execution provide for the use of this distinctive emblem.

Article 37. Denunciation

1. Each High Contracting Party may denounce the present Convention, on its own behalf, or on behalf of any territory for whose international relations it is responsible.

2. The denunciation shall be notified by an instrument in writing, deposited with the Director-General of the United Nations Educational, Scientific and Cultural Organization.

3. The denunciation shall take effect one year after the receipt of the instrument of denunciation. However, if, on the expiry of this period, the denouncing Party is involved in an armed conflict, the denunciation shall not take effect until the end of hostilities, or until the operations of repatriating cultural property are completed, whichever is the later.

Article 38. Notifications

The Director-General of the United Nations Educational, Scientific and Cultural Organization shall inform the States referred to in Articles 30 and 32, as well as the United Nations, of the deposit of all the instruments of ratification, accession or acceptance provided for in Articles 31, 32 and 39 and of the notifications and denunciations provided for respectively in Articles 35, 37 and 39.

Article 39. Revision of the Convention and of the Regulations for its execution

1. Any High Contracting Party may propose amendments to the present Convention or the Regulations for its execution. The text of any proposed amendment shall be communicated to the Director-General of the United Nations Educational, Scientific and Cultural Organization who shall transmit it to each High Contracting Party with the request that such Party reply within four months stating whether it:
(a) desires that a Conference be convened to consider the proposed amendment;
(b) favours the acceptance of the proposed amendment without a Conference; or
(c) favours the rejection of the proposed amendment without a Conference.

2. The Director-General shall transmit the replies, received under paragraph 1 of the present Article, to all High Contracting Parties.

3. If all the High Contracting Parties which have, within the prescribed time-limit, stated their views to the Director-General of the United Nations Educational, Scientific and Cultural Organization, pursuant to paragraph 1(b) of this Article, inform him that they favour acceptance of the amendment without a Conference, notification of their decision shall be made by the

Director-General in accordance with Article 38. The amendment shall become effective for all the High Contracting Parties on the expiry of ninety days from the date of such notification.

4. The Director-General shall convene a Conference of the High Contracting Parties to consider the proposed amendment if requested to do so by more than one-third of the High Contracting Parties.

5. Amendments to the Convention or to the Regulations for its execution, dealt with under the provisions of the preceding paragraph, shall enter into force only after they have been unanimously adopted by the High Contracting Parties represented at the Conference and accepted by each of the High Contracting Parties.

6. Acceptance by the High Contracting Parties of amendments to the Convention or to the Regulations for its execution, which have been adopted by the Conference mentioned in paragraphs 4 and 5, shall be effected by the deposit of a formal instrument with the Director-General of the United Nations Educational, Scientific and Cultural Organization.

7. After the entry into force of amendments to the present Convention or to the Regulations for its execution, only the text of the Convention or of the Regulations for its execution thus amended shall remain open for ratification or accession.

Article 40. Registration

In accordance with Article 102 of the Charter of the United Nations, the present Convention shall be registered with the Secretariat of the United Nations at the request of the Director-General of the United Nations Educational, Scientific and Cultural Organization.

IN FAITH WHEREOF the undersigned, duly authorized, have signed the present Convention.

Done at The Hague, this fourteenth day of May, 1954, in a single copy which shall be deposited in the archives of the United Nations Educational, Scientific and Cultural Organization, and certified true copies of which shall be delivered to all the States referred to in Articles 30 and 32 as well as to the United Nations.

Regulations for the Execution of the Convention for the Protection of Cultural Property in the Event of Armed Conflict

Chapter I. Control

Article 1. International list of persons

On the entry into force of the Convention, the Director-General of the United Nations Educational, Scientific and Cultural Organization shall compile an international list consisting of all persons nominated by the High Contracting Parties as qualified to carry out the functions of Commissioner-General for Cultural Property. On the initiative of the Director-General of the United Nations Educational, Scientific and Cultural Organization, this list shall be periodically revised on the basis of requests formulated by the High Contracting Parties.

Article 2. Organization of control

As soon as any High Contracting Party is engaged in an armed conflict to which Article 18 of the Convention applies:
(a) It shall appoint a representative for cultural property situated in its territory; if it is in occupation of another territory, it shall appoint a special representative for cultural property situated in that territory;
(b) The Protecting Power acting for each of the Parties in conflict with such High Contracting Party shall appoint delegates accredited to the latter in conformity with Article 3 below;
(c) A Commissioner-General for Cultural Property shall be appointed to such High Contracting Party in accordance with Article 4.

Article 3. Appointment of delegates of Protecting Powers

The Protecting Power shall appoint its delegates from among the members of its diplomatic or consular staff or, with the approval of the Party to which they will be accredited, from among other persons.

Article 4. Appointment of Commissioner-General

1. The Commissioner-General for Cultural Property shall be chosen from the international list of persons by joint agreement between the Party to which he will be accredited and the Protecting Powers acting on behalf of the opposing Parties.

2. Should the Parties fail to reach agreement within three weeks from the beginning of their discussions on this point, they shall request the President of the International Court of Justice to appoint the Commissioner-General, who shall not take up his duties until the Party to which he is accredited has approved his appointment.

Article 5. Functions of delegates

The delegates of the Protecting Powers shall take note of violations of the Convention, investigate, with the approval of the Party to which they are accredited, the circumstances in which they have occurred, make representations locally to secure their cessation and, if necessary, notify the Commissioner-General of such violations. They shall keep him informed of their activities.

Article 6. Functions of the Commissioner-General

1. The Commissioner-General for Cultural Property shall deal with all matters referred to him in connexion with the application of the Convention, in conjunction with the representative of the Party to which he is accredited and with the delegates concerned.

2. He shall have powers of decision and appointment in the cases specified in the present Regulations.

3. With the agreement of the Party to which he is accredited, he shall have the right to order an investigation or to conduct it himself.

4. He shall make any representations to the Parties to the conflict or to their Protecting Powers which he deems useful for the application of the Convention.

5. He shall draw up such reports as may be necessary on the application of the Convention and communicate them to the Parties concerned and to their Protecting Powers. He shall send copies to the Director-General of the United Nations Educational, Scientific and Cultural Organization, who may make use only of their technical contents.

6. If there is no Protecting Power, the Commissioner-General shall exercise the functions of the Protecting Power as laid down in Articles 21 and 22 of the Convention.

Article 7. Inspectors and experts

1. Whenever the Commissioner-General for Cultural Property considers it necessary, either at the request of the delegates concerned or after consultation with them, he shall propose, for the approval of the Party to which he is accredited, an inspector of cultural property to be charged with a specific mission. An inspector shall be responsible only to the Commissioner-General.

2. The Commissioner-General, delegates and inspectors may have recourse to the services of experts, who will also be proposed for the approval of the Party mentioned in the preceding paragraph.

Article 8. Discharge of the mission of control

The Commissioners-General for Cultural Property, delegates of the Protecting Powers, inspectors and experts shall in no case exceed their mandates. In particular, they shall take account of the security needs of the High Contracting Party to which they are accredited and shall in all circumstances act in accordance with the requirements of the military situation as communicated to them by that High Contracting Party.

Article 9. Substitutes for Protecting Powers

If a Party to the conflict does not benefit or ceases to benefit from the activities of a Protecting Power, a neutral State may be asked to undertake those functions of a Protecting Power which concern the appointment of a Commissioner-General for Cultural Property in accordance with the procedure laid down in Article 4 above. The Commissioner-General thus appointed shall, if need be, entrust to inspectors the functions of delegates of Protecting Powers as specified in the present Regulations.

Article 10. Expenses

The remuneration and expenses of the Commissioner-General for Cultural Property, inspectors and experts shall be met by the Party to which they are accredited. Remuneration and expenses of delegates of the Protecting Powers shall be subject to agreement between those Powers and the States whose interests they are safeguarding.

Chapter II. Special protection

Article 11. Improvised refuges

1. If, during an armed conflict, any High Contracting Party is induced by unforeseen circumstances to set up an improvised refuge and desires that it should be placed under special protection, it shall communicate this fact forthwith to the Commissioner-General accredited to that Party.

2. If the Commissioner-General considers that such a measure is justified by the circumstances and by the importance of the cultural property sheltered in this improvised refuge, he may authorize the High Contracting Party to display on such refuge the distinctive emblem defined in Article 16 of the Convention. He shall communicate his decision without delay to the delegates of the Protecting Powers who are concerned, each of whom may, within a time-limit of 30 days, order the immediate withdrawal of the emblem.

3. As soon as such delegates have signified their agreement or if the time-limit of 30 days has passed without any of the delegates concerned having made an objection, and if, in the view of the Commissioner-General, the refuge fulfils the conditions laid down in Article 8 of the Convention, the Commissioner-General shall request the Director-General of the United Nations Educational, Scientific and Cultural Organization to enter the refuge in the Register of Cultural Property under Special Protection.

Article 12. International Register of Cultural Property under Special Protection

1. An 'International Register of Cultural Property under Special Protection' shall be prepared.

2. The Director-General of the United Nations Educational, Scientific and Cultural Organization shall maintain this Register. He shall furnish copies to

the Secretary-General of the United Nations and to the High Contracting Parties.

3. The Register shall be divided into sections, each in the name of a High Contracting Party. Each section shall be subdivided into three paragraphs, headed: Refuges, Centres containing Monuments, Other Immovable Cultural Property. The Director-General shall determine what details each section shall contain.

Article 13. Requests for registration

1. Any High Contracting Party may submit to the Director-General of the United Nations Educational, Scientific and Cultural Organization an application for the entry in the Register of certain refuges, centres containing monuments or other immovable cultural property situated within its territory. Such application shall contain a description of the location of such property and shall certify that the property complies with the provisions of Article 8 of the Convention.

2. In the event of occupation, the Occupying Power shall be competent to make such application.

3. The Director-General of the United Nations Educational, Scientific and Cultural Organization shall, without delay, send copies of applications for registration to each of the High Contracting Parties.

Article 14. Objections

1. Any High Contracting Party may, by letter addressed to the Director-General of the United Nations Educational, Scientific and Cultural Organization, lodge an objection to the registration of cultural property. This letter must be received by him within four months of the day on which he sent a copy of the application for registration.

2. Such objection shall state the reasons giving rise to it, the only valid grounds being that:
(a) the property is not cultural property;
(b) the property does not comply with the conditions mentioned in Article 8 of the Convention.

3. The Director-General shall send a copy of the letter of objection to the High Contracting Parties without delay. He shall, if necessary, seek the advice

of the International Committee on Monuments, Artistic and Historical Sites and Archaeological Excavations and also, if he thinks fit, of any other competent organization or person.

4. The Director-General, or the High Contracting Party requesting registration, may make whatever representations they deem necessary to the High Contracting Parties which lodged the objection, with a view to causing the objection to be withdrawn.

5. If a High Contracting Party which has made an application for registration in time of peace becomes involved in an armed conflict before the entry has been made, the cultural property concerned shall at once be provisionally entered in the Register, by the Director-General, pending the confirmation, withdrawal or cancellation of any objection that may be, or may have been, made.

6. If, within a period of six months from the date of receipt of the letter of objection, the Director-General has not received from the High Contracting Party lodging the objection a communication stating that it has been withdrawn, the High Contracting Party applying for registration may request arbitration in accordance with the procedure in the following paragraph.

7. The request for arbitration shall not be made more than one year after the date of receipt by the Director-General of the letter of objection. Each of the two Parties to the dispute shall appoint an arbitrator. When more than one objection has been lodged against an application for registration, the High Contracting Parties which have lodged the objections shall, by common consent, appoint a single arbitrator. These two arbitrators shall select a chief arbitrator from the international list mentioned in Article 1 of the present Regulations. If such arbitrators cannot agree upon their choice, they shall ask the President of the International Court of Justice to appoint a chief arbitrator who need not necessarily be chosen from the international list. The arbitral tribunal thus constituted shall fix its own procedure. There shall be no appeal from its decisions.

8. Each of the High Contracting Parties may declare, whenever a dispute to which it is a Party arises, that it does not wish to apply the arbitration procedure provided for in the preceding paragraph. In such cases, the objection to an application for registration shall be submitted by the Director-General to the High Contracting Parties. The objection will be confirmed only if the High Contracting Parties so decide by a two-third majority of the High Contracting Parties voting. The vote shall be taken by correspondence, unless the Direc-

tor-General of the United Nations Educational, Scientific and Cultural Organization deems it essential to convene a meeting under the powers conferred upon him by Article 27 of the Convention. If the Director-General decides to proceed with the vote by correspondence, he shall invite the High Contracting Parties to transmit their votes by sealed letter within six months from the day on which they were invited to do so.

Article 15. Registration

1. The Director-General of the United Nations Educational, Scientific and Cultural Organization shall cause to be entered in the Register, under a serial number, each item of property for which application for registration is made, provided that he has not received an objection within the time-limit prescribed in paragraph 1 of Article 14.

2. If an objection has been lodged, and without prejudice to the provision of paragraph 5 of Article 14, the Director-General shall enter property in the Register only if the objection has been withdrawn or has failed to be confirmed following the procedures laid down in either paragraph 7 or paragraph 8 of Article 14.

3. Whenever paragraph 3 of Article 11 applies, the Director-General shall enter property in the Register if so requested by the Commissioner-General for Cultural Property.

4. The Director-General shall send without delay to the Secretary-General of the United Nations, to the High Contracting Parties, and, at the request of the Party applying for registration, to all other States referred to in Articles 30 and 32 of the Convention, a certified copy of each entry in the Register. Entries shall become effective thirty days after despatch of such copies.

Article 16. Cancellation

1. The Director-General of the United Nations Educational, Scientific and Cultural Organization shall cause the registration of any property to be cancelled:
(a) at the request of the High Contracting Party within whose territory the cultural property is situated;
(b) if the High Contracting Party which requested registration has denounced the Convention, and when that denunciation has taken effect;
(c) in the special case provided for in Article 14, paragraph 5, when an objection has been confirmed following the procedures mentioned either in paragraph 7 or in paragraph 8 or Article 14.

2.   The Director-General shall send without delay, to the Secretary-General of the United Nations and to all States which received a copy of the entry in the Register, a certified copy of its cancellation. Cancellation shall take effect thirty days after the despatch of such copies.

Chapter III. Transport of cultural property

Article 17. Procedure to obtain immunity

1.   The request mentioned in paragraph 1 of Article 12 of the Convention shall be addressed to the Commissioner-General for Cultural Property. It shall mention the reasons on which it is based and specify the approximate number and the importance of the objects to be transferred, their present location, the location now envisaged, the means of transport to be used, the route to be followed, the date proposed for the transfer, and any other relevant information.

2.   If the Commissioner-General, after taking such opinions as he deems fit, considers that such transfer is justified, he shall consult those delegates of the Protecting Powers who are concerned, on the measures proposed for carrying it out. Following such consultation, he shall notify the Parties to the conflict concerned of the transfer, including in such notification all useful information.

3.   The Commissioner-General shall appoint one or more inspectors, who shall satisfy themselves that only the property stated in the request is to be transferred and that the transport is to be by the approved methods and bears the distinctive emblem. The inspector or inspectors shall accompany the property to its destination.

Article 18. Transport abroad

Where the transfer under special protection is to the territory of another country, it shall be governed not only by Article 12 of the Convention and by Article 17 of the present Regulations, but by the following further provisions:
- (a) while the cultural property remains on the territory of another State, that State shall be its depositary and shall extend to it as great a measure of care as that which it bestows upon its own cultural property of comparable importance;
- (b) the depositary State shall return the property only on the cessation of the conflict; such return shall be effected within six months from the date on which it was requested;

(c) during the various transfer operations, and while it remains on the territory of another State, the cultural property shall be exempt from confiscation and may not be disposed of either by the depositor or by the depositary. Nevertheless, when the safety of the property requires it, the depositary may, with the assent of the depositor, have the property transported to the territory of a third country, under the conditions laid down in the present article;

(d) the request for special protection shall indicate that the State to whose territory the property is to be transferred accepts the provisions of the present Article.

Article 19. Occupied territory

Whenever a High Contracting Party occupying territory of another High Contracting Party transfers cultural property to a refuge situated elsewhere in that territory, without being able to follow the procedure provided for in Article 17 of the Regulations, the transfer in question shall not be regarded as misappropriation within the meaning of Article 4 of the Convention, provided that the Commissioner-General for Cultural Property certifies in writing, after having consulted the usual custodians, that such transfer was rendered necessary by circumstances.

Chapter IV. The distinctive emblem

Article 20. Affixing of the emblem

1. The placing of the distinctive emblem and its degree of visibility shall be left to the discretion of the competent authorities of each High Contracting Party. It may be displayed on flags or armlets; it may be painted on an object or represented in any other appropriate form.

2. However, without prejudice to any possible fuller markings, the emblem shall, in the event of armed conflict and in the cases mentioned in Articles 12 and 13 of the Convention, be placed on the vehicles of transport so as to be clearly visible in daylight from the air as well as from the ground.
The emblem shall be visible from the ground:

(a) at regular intervals sufficient to indicate clearly the perimeter of a centre containing monuments under special protection;

(b) at the entrance to other immovable cultural property under special protection.

Article 21. Identification of persons

1.   The persons mentioned in Article 17, paragraph 2(b) and (c) of the Convention may wear an armlet bearing the distinctive emblem, issued and stamped by the competent authorities.

2.   Such persons shall carry a special identity card bearing the distinctive emblem. This card shall mention at least the surname and first names, the date of birth, the title or rank, and the function of the holder. The card shall bear the photograph of the holder as well as his signature or his fingerprints, or both. It shall bear the embossed stamp of the competent authorities.

3.   Each High Contracting Party shall make out its own type of identity card, guided by the model annexed, by way of example, to the present Regulations. The High Contracting Parties shall transmit to each other a specimen of the model they are using. Identity cards shall be made out, if possible, at least in duplicate, one copy being kept by the issuing Power.

4.   The said persons may not, without legitimate reason, be deprived of their identity card or of the right to wear the armlet.

Front

IDENTITY CARD

for personnel engaged in the
protection of cultural property

Surname ....

First names ....

Date of Birth..

Title or Rank..

Function ....

is the bearer of this card under the terms of the Convention of The Hague, dated 14 May, 1954, for the Protection of Cultural Property in the event of Armed Conflict.

Date of Issue   **Number of Card**

....

Reverse side

Photo of bearer

Signature of bearer or fingerprints or both

Embossed stamp of authority issuing card

Height	Eyes	Hair

Other distinguishing marks

....

....

....

....

....

....

....

Protocol

The High Contracting Parties are agreed as follows:

I

1. Each High Contracting Party undertakes to prevent the exportation, from a territory occupied by it during an armed conflict, of cultural property as defined in Article 1 of the Convention for the Protection of Cultural Property in the Event of Armed Conflict, signed at The Hague on 14 May, 1954.

2. Each High Contracting Party undertakes to take into its custody cultural property imported into its territory either directly or indirectly from any occupied territory. This shall either be effected automatically upon the importation of the property or, failing this, at the request of the authorities of that territory.

3. Each High Contracting Party undertakes to return, at the close of hostilities, to the competent authorities of the territory previously occupied, cultural property which is in its territory, if such property has been exported in contravention of the principle laid down in the first paragraph. Such property shall never be retained as war reparations.

4. The High Contracting Party whose obligation it was to prevent the exportation of cultural property from the territory occupied by it, shall pay an indemnity to the holders in good faith of any cultural property which has to be returned in accordance with the preceding paragraph.

II

5. Cultural property coming from the territory of a High Contracting Party and deposited by it in the territory of another High Contracting Party for the purpose of protecting such property against the dangers of an armed conflict, shall be returned by the latter, at the end of hostilities, to the competent authorities of the territory from which it came.

III

6. The present Protocol shall bear the date of 14 May, 1954 and, until the date of 31 December, 1954, shall remain open for signature by all States invited to the Conference which met at The Hague from 21 April, 1954 to 14 May, 1954.

7. (a) The present Protocol shall be subject to ratification by signatory States in accordance with their respective constitutional procedures.

(b) The instruments of ratification shall be deposited with the Director-General of the United Nations Educational, Scientific and Cultural Organization.

8. From the date of its entry into force, the present Protocol shall be open for accession by all States mentioned in paragraph 6 which have not signed it as well as any other State invited to accede by the Executive Board of the United Nations Educational, Scientific and Cultural Organization. Accession shall be effected by the deposit of an instrument of accession with the Director-General of the United Nations Educational, Scientific and Cultural Organization.

9. The States referred to in paragraphs 6 and 8 may declare, at the time of signature, ratification or accession, that they will not be bound by the provisions of Section I or by those of Section II of the present Protocol.

10. (a) The present Protocol shall enter into force three months after five instruments of ratification have been deposited.

(b) Thereafter, it shall enter into force, for each High Contracting Party, three months after the deposit of its instrument of ratification or accession.

(c) The situations referred to in Articles 18 and 19 of the Convention for the Protection of Cultural Property in the Event of Armed Conflict, signed at The Hague on 14 May, 1954, shall give immediate effect to ratifications and accessions deposited by the Parties to the conflict either before or after the beginning of hostilities or occupation. In such cases, the Director-General of the United Nations Educational, Scientific and Cultural Organization shall transmit the communications referred to in paragraph 14 by the speediest method.

11. (a) Each State Party to the Protocol on the date of its entry into force shall take all necessary measures to ensure its effective application within a period of six months after such entry into force.

(b) This period shall be six months from the date of deposit of the instruments of ratification or accession for any State which deposits its instrument of ratification or accession after the date of the entry into force of the Protocol.

12. Any High Contracting Party may, at the time of ratification or accession, or at any time thereafter, declare by notification addressed to the Director-General of the United Nations Educational, Scientific and Cultural Organization, that the present Protocol shall extend to all or any of the territories for whose international relations it is responsible. The said notification shall take effect three months after the date of its receipt.

13. (a) Each High Contracting Party may denounce the present Protocol, on its own behalf, or on behalf of any territory for whose international relations it is responsible.

(b) The denunciation shall be notified by an instrument in writing, deposited with the Director-General of the United Nations Educational, Scientific and Cultural Organization.

(c) The denunciation shall take effect one year after receipt of the instrument of denunciation. However, if, on the expiry of this period, the denouncing Party is involved in an armed conflict, the denunciation shall not take effect until the end of hostilities, or until the operations of repatriating cultural property are completed, whichever is the later.

14. The Director-General of the United Nations Educational, Scientific and Cultural Organization shall inform the States referred to in paragraphs 6 and 8, as well as the United Nations, of the deposit of all the instruments of ratification, accession or acceptance provided for in paragraphs 7, 8 and 15 and the notifications and denunciations provided for respectively in paragraphs 12 and 13.

15. (a) The present Protocol may be revised if revision is requested by more than one-third of the High Contracting Parties.

(b) The Director-General of the United Nations Educational, Scientific and Cultural Organization shall convene a Conference for this purpose.

IV.A.3

(c) Amendments to the present Protocol shall enter into force only after they have been unanimously adopted by the High Contracting Parties represented at the Conference and accepted by each of the High Contracting Parties.

(d) Acceptance by the High Contracting Parties of amendments to the present Protocol, which have been adopted by the Conference mentioned in sub-paragraphs (b) and (c), shall be effected by the deposit of a formal instrument with the Director-General of the United Nations Educational, Scientific and Cultural Organization.

(e) After the entry into force of amendments to the present Protocol, only the text of the said Protocol thus amended shall remain open for ratification or accession.

In accordance with Article 102 of the Charter of the United Nations, the present Protocol shall be registered with the Secretariat of the United Nations at the request of the Director-General of the United Nations Educational, Scientific and Cultural Organization.

In faith whereof the undersigned, duly authorized, have signed the present Protocol.

Done at The Hague, this fourteenth day of May, 1954, in English, French, Russian and Spanish, the four texts being equally authoritative, in a single copy which shall be deposited in the archives of the United Nations Educational, Scientific and Cultural Organization, and certified true copies of which shall be delivered to all the States referred to in paragraphs 6 and 8 as well as to the United Nations.

Resolutions

Resolution I

The Conference expresses the hope that the competent organs of the United Nations should decide, in the event of military action being taken in implementation of the Charter, to ensure application of the provisions of the Convention by the armed forces taking part in such action.

Resolution II

The Conference expresses the hope that each of the High Contracting Parties, on acceding to the Convention, should set up, within the framework of its constitutional and administrative system, a national advisory committee consisting of a small number of distinguished persons: for example, senior officials of archaeological services, museums, etc., a representative of the military general staff, a representative of the Ministry of Foreign Affairs a specialist in international law and two or three other members whose official duties or specialized knowledge are related to the fields covered by the Convention.

The Committee should be under the authority of the minister of State or senior official responsible for the national service chiefly concerned with the care of cultural property. Its chief functions would be:

(a) to advise the government concerning the measures required for the implementation of the Convention in its legislative, technical or military aspects, both in time of peace and during an armed conflict;

(b) to approach its government in the event of an armed conflict or when such a conflict appears imminent, with a view to ensuring that cultural property situated within its own territory or within that of other countries is known

IV.A.3

to, and respected and protected by the armed forces of the country, in accordance with the provisions of the Convention;

(c) to arrange, in agreement with its government, for liaison and co-operation with other similar national committees and with any competent international authority.

Resolution III

The Conference expresses the hope that the Director-General of the United Nations Educational, Scientific and Cultural Organization should convene, as soon as possible after the entry into force of the Convention for the Protection of Cultural Property in the Event of Armed Conflict, a meeting of the High Contracting Parties.

IV.A.3

State of ratifications (R) and accessions (a) as at 31 October 1984

Depositary: Unesco
Open for signature: from 14 May to 31 December 1954[1]
Entry into force: 7 August 1956, in accordance with Article 33
Authoritative texts: English, French, Russian, Spanish
Registration at the Secretariat of the United Nations:
    4 September 1956, No. 3511

	Date of deposit of instrument		
	Convention	*Protocol*	*Sections*
Albania	20 December 1960 a	20 December 1960 a	I, II
Australia	19 September 1984 R		
Austria	25 March 1964 R	25 March 1964 R	I, II
Belgium	16 September 1960 R	16 September 1960 R	I, II
Brazil	12 September 1958 R	12 September 1958 R	I, II
Bulgaria	7 August 1956 a	9 October 1958 a	I, II
Burkina Faso	18 December 1969 a		
Burma	10 February 1956 R	10 February 1956 R	I, II
Byelorussian Soviet Socialist Republic	7 May 1957 R	7 May 1957 R	I, II
Cameroon	12 October 1961 a	12 October 1961 a	I, II
Cuba	26 November 1957 R	26 November 1957 R	I, II
Cyprus	9 September 1964 a	9 September 1964 a	I, II
Czechoslovakia	6 December 1957 R	6 December 1957 R	I, II
Democratic Kampuchea	4 April 1962 R	4 April 1962 R	I, II
Democratic Yemen	6 February 1970 a	6 February 1970 a	I, II
Dominican Republic	5 January 1960 a		
Ecuador	2 October 1956 R	8 February 1961 R	I, II
Egypt	17 August 1955 R	17 August 1955 R	I, II
France	7 June 1957 R	7 June 1957 R	I, II
Gabon	4 December 1961 a	4 December 1961 a	I, II
German Democratic Republic	16 January 1974 a	16 January 1974 a	I, II

	Date of deposit of instrument		
	Convention	*Protocol*	*Sections*
Germany, Federal Republic of[2]	11 August 1967 R	11 August 1967 R	I, II
Ghana	25 July 1960 a	25 July 1960 a	I, II
Greece	9 February 1981 R	9 February 1981 R	I, II
Guinea	20 September 1960 a	11 December 1961 a	I, II
Holy See	24 February 1958 a	24 February 1958 a	I, II
Hungary	17 May 1956 R	16 August 1956 a	I, II
India	16 June 1958 R	16 June 1958 R	I, II
Indonesia	10 January 1967 R	26 July 1967 R	I, II
Iran	22 June 1959 R	22 June 1959 R	I, II
Iraq	21 December 1967 R	21 December 1967 R	I, II
Israel	3 October 1957 R	1 April 1958 a	I, II
Italy	9 May 1958 R	9 May 1958 R	I, II
Ivory Coast	24 January 1980 a		
Jordan	2 October 1957 R	2 October 1957 R	I, II
Kuwait	6 June 1969 a	11 February 1970 a	I, II
Lebanon	1 June 1960 R	1 June 1960 R	I, II
Libyan Arab Jamahiriya	19 November 1957 R	19 November 1957 R	I, II
Liechtenstein	28 April 1960 a	28 April 1960 a	I, II
Luxembourg	29 September 1961 R	29 September 1961 R	I, II
Madagascar	3 November 1961 a	3 November 1961 a	I, II
Malaysia	12 December 1960 a	12 December 1960 a	I, II
Mali	18 May 1961 a	18 May 1961 a	I, II
Mexico	7 May 1956 R	7 May 1956 R	I, II
Monaco	10 December 1957 R	10 December 1957 R	I, II
Mongolia	4 November 1964 a		
Morocco	30 August 1968 a	30 August 1968 a	I, II
Netherlands	14 October 1958 R	14 October 1958 R	I, II
Nicaragua	25 November 1959 R	25 November 1959 R	I, II
Niger	6 December 1976 a	6 December 1976 a	I, II
Nigeria	5 June 1961 a	5 June 1961 a	I, II
Norway	19 September 1961 R	19 September 1961 R	I, II
Oman	26 October 1977 a		
Pakistan	27 March 1959 a	27 March 1959 a	I, II
Panama	17 July 1962 a		
Poland	6 August 1956 R	6 August 1956 R	I, II
Qatar	31 July 1973 a		
Romania	21 March 1958 R	21 March 1958 a	I, II
San Marino	9 February 1956 R	9 February 1956 R	I, II
Saudi Arabia	20 January 1971 a		

IV.A.3.Ratif.

| | Date of deposit of instrument | | |
	Convention	Protocol	Sections
Spain	7 July 1960 R		
Sudan	23 July 1970 a		
Switzerland	15 May 1962 a	15 May 1962 a	I, II
Syrian Arab Republic	6 March 1958 R	6 March 1958 R	I, II
Thailand	2 May 1958 a	2 May 1958 a	I, II
Tunisia	28 January 1981 a	28 January 1981 a	I, II
Turkey	15 December 1965 a	15 December 1965 a	I, II
Ukrainian Soviet Socialist Republic	6 February 1957 R	6 February 1957 R	I, II
Union of Soviet Socialist Republics	4 January 1957 R	4 January 1957 R	I, II
United Republic of Tanzania	23 September 1971 a		
Yugoslavia	13 February 1956 R	13 February 1956 R	I, II
Zaire	18 April 1961 a	18 April 1961 a	I, II

Notes

1. The Convention has been signed by the following States: Andorra,* Australia (14 May 1954); Austria (31 December 1954); Belgium (14 May 1954); Brazil, Burma (31 December 1954); Byelorussian Soviet Socialist Republic (30 December 1954); [China],** Cuba (14 May 1954); Czechoslovakia (18 October 1954); Democratic Kampuchea (17 December 1954); Denmark (18 October 1954); Ecuador, Egypt (30 December 1954); El Salvador, France, Germany (Federal Republic of), Greece, Hungary, India (14 May 1954); Indonesia (24 December 1954); Iran, Iraq, Ireland, Israel, Italy, (14 May 1954); Japan (6 September 1954); Jordan (22 December 1954); Lebanon (25 May 1954); Libyan Arab Jamahiriya, Luxembourg (14 May 1954); Mexico (29 December 1954); Monaco, Nicaragua, Norway (14 May 1954); New Zealand (20 December 1954); Netherlands, Philippines, Poland, Portugal, Romania (14 May 1954); San Marino, Spain, Syrian Arab Republic, Ukrainian Soviet Socialist Republic, United Kingdom (30 December 1954); Union of Soviet Socialist Republics, United States of America, Uruguay, Yugoslavia (14 May 1954).

   The Protocol has been signed by the same States, except for the following: Andorra, Australia, Hungary, Ireland, Israel, New Zealand, Portugal, Romania, United Kingdom, United States of America.

*   Signed on behalf of the Bishop of Urgel, co-prince of Andorra. The French Minister of Foreign Affairs, by a communication dated 5 August 1954, made it known that the President of the French Republic, co-prince of Andorra, considered that signature as null and void, the French State alone being empowered to represent the Andorran interests on an international level (see letter CL/996 of 22 October 1954). The Bishop of Urgel, by letter of 6 December 1954, replied to this communication, calling attention to his position as a sovereign co-prince (see letter CL/1026 of 22 February 1955).

**   Signed on behalf of China by its representatives to the United Nations and Unesco at the time of signature.

China is an original Member of the United Nations, the Charter having been signed and ratified in its name, on 26 and 28 September 1945, respectively, by the Government of the Republic of China, which continuously represented China in the United Nations until 25 October 1971.

China is likewise an original Member of Unesco, the Constitution having been signed and accepted in its name by the Government of the Republic of China which continuously represented China in Unesco until 29 October 1971.

On 25 October 1971, the General Assembly of the United Nations adopted Resolution 2758(XXVI), which reads as follows:

'*The General Assembly,*

'*Recalling* the principles of the Charter of the United Nations,

'*Considering* that the restoration of the lawful rights of the People's Republic of China is essential both for the protection of the Charter of the United Nations and for the cause that the United Nations must serve under the Charter,

'*Recognizing* that the representatives of the Government of the People's Republic of China are the only lawful representatives of China to the United Nations and that the People's Republic of China is one of the five permanent members of the Security Council,

'*Decides* to restore all its rights to the People's Republic of China and to recognize the representatives of its Government as the only legitimate representatives of China to the United Nations, and to expel forthwith the representatives of Chiang Kai-shek from the place which they unlawfully occupy at the United Nations and in all the organizations related to it.'

The establishing of the Government of the People's Republic of China, occurring on 1 October 1949, was made known to the United Nations on 18 November 1949. Various proposals were formulated between that date and that of the adoption of the above-quoted resolution with a view to changing the representation of China at the United Nations, but these proposals were not adopted.

On 29 October 1971, the Executive Board of Unesco, at its 88th session, adopted the following decision (88 EX/Decision 9):

'The Executive Board,

'1.   *Taking into account* the resolution adopted by the United Nations General Assembly on 25 October 1971, whereby the representatives of the People's Republic of China were recognized as the only lawful representatives of China to the United Nations,

'2.   *Recalling* resolution 396 adopted by the United Nations General Assembly at its fifth regular session on 14 December 1950 recommending that "the attitude adopted by the General Assembly" on the question of the representation of a Member State "should be taken into account in other organs of the United Nations and in the Specialized Agencies".

                                                 IV.A.2.Ratif. 4

'3.   *Decides* that, from today onwards, the Government of the People's Republic of China is the only legitimate representative of China in Unesco and *invites* the Director-General to act accordingly.'

On 29 September 1972 the Secretary-General of the United Nations received the following communication from the Minister of Foreign Affairs of the People's Republic of China (translation):

'1.   As concerns the multilateral treaties which the defunct Chinese Government signed, ratified or acceded to before the establishing of the Government of the People's Republic of China, my government will examine their terms before deciding, in the light of circumstances, whether they should or not be recognized.

'2.   As from 1 October 1949, day of the founding of the People's Republic of China, the Chiang Kai-shek clique has no right to represent China. Its signing and ratifying of any multilateral treaty, or its acceding to any multilateral treaty, by usurping the name of "China", are all illegal and void. My government will study these multilateral treaties before deciding, in the light of circumstances, whether it is or is not appropriate to accede to them.'

On depositing the instrument of acceptance of the Agreement, the Government of Romania stated that it considered the above-mentioned signature as null and void, inasmuch as the only Government competent to assume obligations on behalf of China and to represent China at the international level is the Government of the People's Republic of China.

In a letter addressed to the Secretary-General in regard to the above-mentioned declaration, the Permanent Representative of the Republic of China to the United Nations stated: 'The Republic of China, a sovereign State and member of the United Nations, attended the Fifth Session of the General Conference of the United Nations Educational, Cultural and Scientific Organization, contributed to the formulation of the Agreement on the Importation of Educational, Scientific and Cultural Materials and duly signed the said Agreement on 22 November 1950 at the Interim Headquarters of the United Nations at Lake Success. Any statement relating to the said Agreement that is incompatible with or derogatory to the legitimate position of the Government of the Republic of China shall in no way affect the rights and obligations of the Republic of China as a signatory of the said Agreement.'

2.   With notification by the Government of the Federal Republic of Germany declaring that the Convention and Protocol will also apply to the *Land* of Berlin with effect from the date on which the Convention and Protocol enter into force for the Federal Republic of Germany. (See letter CL/1904 of 26 September 1967.)

This notification involved communications from the following States:

Union of Soviet Socialist Republics (16 October 1967), Ukrainian Soviet Socialist Republic (23 October 1967), Byelorussian Soviet Socialist Republic (31 October 1967); Poland (27 December 1967); Romania (29 December 1967); Bulgaria (27 May 1969). These communications are identical in essence to those referred to on pages I.A.1. Ratif 5,* namely that the above-mentioned declarations have no legal effect since Berlin (West) has never been and is not a part of the Federal Republic of Germany. (See letters CL/1926 of 29 February 1968 and CL/2043 of 25 August 1969.)

Federal Republic of Germany (4 April 1968): 'The Convention and Protocol will also apply to the *Land* of Berlin with effect from the date on which the Convention and Protocol enter into force for the Federal Republic of Germany, account being taken of the rights and responsibilities of the Allied Authorities, in particular the powers retained by them with regard to the maintenance of the security of Berlin and, notably, those in the military field.' (See letter CL/1948 of 17 June 1968.)

Union of Soviet Socialist Republics (15 July 1968), Ukrainian Soviet Socialist Republic (23 July 1968), Byelorussian Soviet Socialist Republic (29 July 1968). In regard to this last communication of the Federal Republic of Germany of 4 April 1968, these States re-affirmed, in substance, their position previously adopted. (See letter CL/1985 of 20 November 1968.)

Federal Republic of Germany, United States of America, United Kingdom (5 September 1968). The communications of these States (letter CL/1984 of 25 November 1968) are substantially identical to those reproduced on page I.A.I, Ratif. 7,* under 'France'. (Letter CL/2112 of 6 November 1970).

Union of Soviet Socialist Republics (24 December 1968), Ukrainian Soviet Socialist Republic (8 January 1969), Byelorussian Soviet Socialist Republic (10 January 1969). These States reaffirmed their position previously adopted (see letter CL/2018 of 24 April 1969).

Federal Republic of Germany, France, United Kingdom, United States of America (10 September 1970). The text of this communication (letter CL/2112 of 6 November 1970) is on page I.A.1, Ratif. 5,* under 'France'.

Union of Soviet Socialist Republics, Ukrainian Soviet Socialist Republic, Byelorussian Soviet Socialist Republic (18 January 1971). The text of this communication (letter CL/2141 of 29 April 1971) is on page I.A.1. Ratif. 6.*

German Democratic Republic (15 December 1973). In substance this communication (letter CL/2351 Add. of 14 August 1974) is identical with that on page I.A.1. Ratif. 8* (letter CL/2399 of 6 September 1974).

United Kingdom, France (28 April 1975), United States of America (28 May 1975). The texts of these communications (letter CL/2484 of 1 October 1975) are reproduced on page I.A.1. Ratif 6.*

___

* See *Unesco's Standard-setting Instruments.*

Declarations and reservations

Byelorussian Soviet Socialist Republic [at signature of the Convention]
The representative of the Byelorussian Soviet Socialist Republic noted that 'various provisions included in the Convention and Regulations weaken these agreements with regard to the conservation and defence of cultural property in the event of armed conflict and that, for that reason, he could not express his satisfaction'. (See *Acts of the Hague Conference, Records*, para. 2215.) Similar declarations were made at the same time by the Ukrainian Soviet Socialist Republic and the Union of Soviet Socialist Republics (ibid., paras. 2216-17).

Germany (Federal Republic of)
'As, however, . . . ratification will take some time, owing to the federal character of the Federal Republic of Germany, . . . in accordance with Article 18(3) of the above-mentioned Convention, . . . the Federal Republic of Germany accepts and applies the provisions of the said Convention . . . accordingly, under the above-mentioned Article 18(3), all other Parties to the said Convention are thereby bound in relation to the Federal Republic of Germany.' (See letter ODG/SJ/2/467 of 2 May 1962.)

Norway
(Translation) '. . . the restitution of cultural property, in accordance with the terms of Sections I and II of the Protocol, can be demanded only after the expiration of a period of 20 years after the date on which the property in question came into the possession of a good-faith holder.' (See letter CL/1522 of 30 October 1961.)*

Sudan
'In view of the fact that it considers that the Royal Government of the National Union of Cambodia, of Samdeck Norodom Sihanouk is the only Government empowered to represent the Kingdom of Cambodia, it follows that the Government of the Democratic Republic of Sudan does not recognize the right of the Phnom-Penh regime to enter into international obligations on behalf of the Kingdom of Cambodia.' (See letter CL/2236 of 18 October 1972.)

---

* Bulgaria, Byelorussian Soviet Socialist Republic, Chad, Czechoslovakia, German Democratic Republic, India, Italy, Madagascar, Mexico, Netherlands, Poland, Romania, San Marino, Spain, United Arab Republic and Union of Soviet Socialist Republics issued observations as regards this reservation (see letters CL/1606 of 27 November 1962 and CL/2351 Add. of 14 August 1974).
By a *note verbale* dated 3 October 1973, Norway announced its decision, effective 24 August 1979, to withdraw that reservation (see letter LA/Depositary/1979/23 of 6 December 1979).

Convention on the Means of Prohibiting and Preventing the Illicit Import, Export and Transfer of Ownership of Cultural Property [1]

Introduction

The purpose of this Convention is to develop the principles and standards set forth in the Recommendation on the same subject adopted by the General Conference in 1964 and to make them binding on the States which are Contracting Parties thereto.

It defines at length cultural property qualifying for protection not only on historical, archaeological or artistic grounds, but in the interests of science as well.

The transfer of ownership, import and export of all the property covered by this definition is not automatically prohibited. It is for each State Party to the Convention to establish regulations regarding operations that affect property situated in its territory and to decide which are licit and which are illicit.

The States Parties to the Convention undertake to adopt the necessary measures: (a) to prevent museums within their territories from acquiring cultural property which has been illegally exported; (b) to prohibit the import of cultural property stolen from a museum or a public institution after the entry into force of the Convention; (c) at the request of the State of origin, to recover and return any such cultural property stolen and imported.

The Convention came into force on 24 April 1972.

---

1. Adopted on 14 November 1970 by the General Conference of Unesco at the sixteenth session, held in Paris.

IV.A.4. Intro.

United Nations Educational, Scientific and
Cultural Organization

Convention on the Means of Prohibiting
and Preventing the Illicit Import, Export and Transfer
of Ownership of Cultural Property

Adopted by the General Conference at its
sixteenth session, Paris, 14 November 1970

The General Conference of the United Nations Educational, Scientific and Cultural Organization, meeting in Paris from 12 October to 14 November 1970, at its sixteenth session,

Recalling the importance of the provisions contained in the Declaration of the Principles of International Cultural Co-operation, adopted by the General Conference at its fourteenth session,

Considering that the interchange of cultural property among nations for scientific, cultural and educational purposes increases the knowledge of the civilization of Man, enriches the cultural life of all peoples and inspires mutual respect and appreciation among nations,

Considering that cultural property constitutes one of the basic elements of civilization and national culture, and that its true value can be appreciated only in relation to the fullest possible information regarding is origin, history and traditional setting,

Considering that it is incumbent upon every State to protect the cultural property existing within its territory against the dangers of theft, clandestine excavation, and illicit export,

Considering that, to avert these dangers, it is essential for every State to become increasingly alive to the moral obligations to respect its own cultural heritage and that of all nations,

Considering that, as cultural institutions, museums, libraries and archives should ensure that their collections are built up in accordance with universally recognized moral principles,

Considering that the illicit import, export and transfer of ownership of cultural property is an obstacle to that understanding between nations which it is part of Unesco's mission to promote by recommending to interested States, international conventions to this end,

IV.A.4

Considering that the protection of cultural heritage can be effective only if organized both nationally and internationally among States working in close co-operation,

Considering that the Unesco General Conference adopted a Recommendation to this effect in 1964,

Having before it further proposals on the means of prohibiting and preventing the illicit import, export and transfer of ownership of cultural property, a question which is on the agenda for the session as item 19.

Having decided, at its fifteenth session, that this question should be made the subject of an international convention,

Adopts this Convention on the fourteenth day of November 1970.

Article 1

For the purposes of this Convention, the term 'cultural property' means property which, on religious or secular grounds, is specifically designated by each State as being of importance for archaeology, prehistory, history, literature, art or science and which belongs to the following categories:

(a) Rare collections and specimens of fauna, flora, minerals and anatomy, and objects of palaeontological interest;

(b) property relating to history, including the history of science and technology and military and social history, to the life of national leaders, thinkers, scientists and artists and to events of national importance;

(c) products of archaeological excavations (including regular and clandestine) or of archaeological discoveries;

(d) elements of artistic or historical monuments or archaeological sites which have been dismembered;

(e) antiquities more than one hundred years old, such as inscriptions, coins and engraved seals;

(f) objects of ethnological interest;

(g) property of artistic interest, such as:

    (i) pictures, paintings and drawings produced entirely by hand on any support and in any material (excluding industrial designs and manufactured articles decorated by hand);

    (ii) original works of statuary art and sculpture in any material;

    (iii) original engravings, prints and lithographs;

    (iv) original artistic assemblages and montages in any material;

(h) rare manuscripts and incunabula, old books, documents and publications of special interest (historical, artistic, scientific, literary, etc.) singly or in collections;

(i) postage, revenue and similar stamps, singly or in collections;

(j) archives, including sound, photographic and cinematographic archives;

(k) articles of furniture more than one hundred years old and old musical instruments.

Article 2

1. The States Parties to this Convention recognize that the illicit import, export and transfer of ownership of cultural property is one of the main causes of the impoverishment of the cultural heritage of the countries of origin of such property and that international co-operation constitutes one of the most efficient means of protecting each country's cultural property against all the dangers resulting therefrom.

2. To this end, the States Parties undertake to oppose such practices with the means at their disposal, and particularly by removing their causes, putting a stop to current practices, and by helping to make the necessary reparations.

Article 3

The import, export or transfer of ownership of cultural property effected contrary to the provisions adopted under this Convention by the States Parties thereto, shall be illicit.

Article 4

The States Parties to this Convention recognize that for the purpose of the Convention property which belongs to the following categories forms part of the cultural heritage of each State:
(a) Cultural property created by the individual or collective genius of nationals of the State concerned, and cultural property of importance to the State concerned created within the territory of that State by foreign nationals or stateless persons resident within such territory;
(b) cultural property found within the national territory;
(c) cultural property acquired by archaeological, ethnological or natural science missions, with the consent of the competent authorities of the country of origin of such property;
(d) cultural property which has been the subject of a freely agreed exchange;
(e) cultural property received as a gift or purchased legally with the consent of the competent authorities of the country of origin of such property.

Article 5

To ensure the protection of their cultural property against illicit import, export and transfer of ownership, the States Parties to this Convention undertake, as appropriate for each country, to set up within their territories one or more national services, where such services do not already exist, for the protection of the cultural heritage, with a qualified staff sufficient in number for the effective carrying out of the following functions:

(a) contributing to the formation of draft laws and regulations designed to secure the protection of the cultural heritage and particularly prevention of the illicit import, export and transfer of ownership of important cultural property;

(b) establishing and keeping up to date, on the basis of a national inventory of protected property, a list of important public and private cultural property whose export would constitute an appreciable impoverishment of the national cultural heritage;

(c) promoting the development or the establishment of scientific and technical institutions (museums, libraries, archives, laboratories, workshops . . .) required to ensure the preservation and presentation of cultural property;

(d) organizing the supervision of archaeological excavations, ensuring the preservation 'in situ' of certain cultural property, and protecting certain areas reserved for future archaeological research;

(e) establishing, for the benefit of those concerned (curators, collectors, antique dealers, etc.) rules in conformity with the ethical principles set forth in this Convention; and taking steps to ensure the observance of those rules;

(f) taking educational measures to stimulate and develop respect for the cultural heritage of all States, and spreading knowledge of the provisions of this Convention;

(g) seeing that appropriate publicity is given to the disappearance of any items of cultural property.

Article 6

The States Parties to this Convention undertake:

(a) To introduce an appropriate certificate in which the exporting State would specify that the export of the cultural property in question is authorized. The certificate should accompany all items of cultural property exported in accordance with the regulations;

(b) to prohibit the exportation of cultural property from their territory unless accompanied by the above-mentioned export certificate;

(c) to publicize this prohibition by appropriate means, particularly among persons likely to export or import cultural property.

Article 7

The States Parties to this Convention undertake:

(a) To take the necessary measures, consistent with national legislation, to prevent museums and similar institutions within their territories from acquiring cultural property originating in another State Party which has been illegally exported after entry into force of this Convention, in the States concerned. Whenever possible, to inform a State of origin Party to this Convention of an offer of such cultural property illegally removed from that State after the entry into force of this Convention in both States;

(b) (i) to prohibit the import of cultural property stolen from a museum or a religious or secular public monument or similar institution in another State Party to this Convention after the entry into force of this Convention for the States concerned, provided that such property is documented as appertaining to the inventory of that institution;

(ii) at the request of the State Party of origin, to take appropriate steps to recover and return any such cultural property imported after the entry into force of this Convention in both States concerned, provided, however, that the requesting State shall pay just compensation to an innocent purchaser or to a person who has valid title to that property. Requests for recovery and return shall be made through diplomatic offices. The requesting Party shall furnish, at its expense, the documentation and other evidence necessary to establish its claim for recovery and return. The Parties shall impose no customs duties or other charges upon cultural property returned pursuant to this Article. All expenses incident to the return and delivery of the cultural property shall be borne by the requesting Party.

Article 8

The States Parties to this Convention undertake to impose penalties or administrative sanctions on any person responsible for infringing the prohibitions referred to under Articles 6(b) and 7(b) above.

Article 9

Any State Party to this Convention whose cultural patrimony is in jeopardy from pillage of archaeological or ethnological materials may call upon other States Parties who are affected. The States Parties to this Convention undertake, in these circumstances, to participate in a concerted international effort to determine and to carry out the necessary concrete measures, including the control of exports and imports and international commerce in the specific materials concerned. Pending agreement each State concerned shall take provisional measures to the extent feasible to prevent irremediable injury to the cultural heritage of the requesting State.

Article 10

The States Parties to this Convention undertake:

(a) To restrict by education, information and vigilance, movement of cultural property illegally removed from any State Party to this Convention and, as appropriate for each country, oblige antique dealers, subject to penal or administrative sanctions, to maintain a register recording the origin of each item of cultural property, names and addresses of the supplier, description and price of each item sold and to inform the purchaser of the cultural property of the export prohibition to which such property may be subject;

(b) to endeavour by educational means to create and develop in the public mind a realization of the value of cultural property and the threat to the cultural heritage created by theft, clandestine excavations and illicit exports.

Article 11

The export and transfer of ownership of cultural property under compulsion arising directly or indirectly from the occupation of a country by a foreign power shall be regarded as illicit.

Article 12

The States Parties to this Convention shall respect the cultural heritage within the territories for the international relations of which they are responsible, and shall take all appropriate measures to prohibit and prevent the illicit import, export and transfer of ownership of cultural property in such territories.

Article 13

The States Parties to this Convention also undertake, consistent with the laws of each State:

(a) To prevent by all appropriate means transfers of ownership of cultural property likely to promote the illicit import or export of such property;

(b) to ensure that their competent services co-operate in facilitating the earliest possible restitution of illicitly exported cultural property to its rightful owner;

(c) to admit actions for recovery of lost or stolen items of cultural property brought by or on behalf of the rightful owners;

(d) to recognize the indefeasible right of each State Party to this Convention to classify and declare certain cultural property as inalienable which should therefore *ipso facto* not be exported, and to facilitate recovery of such property by the State concerned in cases where it has been exported.

Article 14

In order to prevent illicit export and to meet the obligations arising from the implementation of this Convention, each State Party to the Convention should, as far as it is able, provide the national services responsible for the protection of its cultural heritage with an adequate budget and, if necessary, should set up a fund for this purpose.

Article 15

Nothing in this Convention shall prevent States Parties thereto from concluding special agreements among themselves or from continuing to implement agreements already concluded regarding the restitution of cultural property removed, whatever the reason, from its territory of origin, before the entry into force of this Convention for the States concerned.

Article 16

The States Parties to this Convention shall in their periodic reports submitted to the General Conference of the United Nations Educational, Scientific and Cultural Organization on dates and in a manner to be determined by it, give information on the legislative and administrative provisions which they have adopted and other action which they have taken for the application of this Convention, together with details of the experience acquired in this field.

Article 17

1. The States Parties to this Convention may call on the technical assistance of the United Nations Educational, Scientific and Cultural Organization, particularly as regards:
(a) Information and education;
(b) consultation and expert advice;
(c) co-ordination and good offices.

2. The United Nations Educational, Scientific and Cultural Organization may, on its own initiative conduct research and publish studies on matters relevant to the illicit movement of cultural property.

3. To this end, the United Nations Educational, Scientific and Cultural Organization may also call on the co-operation of any competent non-governmental organization.

4. The United Nations Educational, Scientific and Cultural Organization may, on its own initiative, make proposals to States Parties to this Convention for its implementation.

5. At the request of at least two States Parties to this Convention which are engaged in a dispute over its implementation, Unesco may extend its good offices to reach a settlement between them.

Article 18

This Convention is drawn up in English, French, Russian and Spanish, the four texts being equally authoritative.

Article 19

1. This Convention shall be subject to ratification or acceptance by States members of the United Nations Educational, Scientific and Cultural Organization in accordance with their respective constitutional procedures.

2. The instruments of ratification or acceptance shall be deposited with the Director-General of the United Nations Educational, Scientific and Cultural Organization.

Article 20

1. This Convention shall be open to accession by all States not members of the United Nations Educational, Scientific and Cultural Organization which are invited to accede to it by the Executive Board of the Organization.

2. Accession shall be effected by the deposit of an instrument of accession with the Director-General of the United Nations Educational, Scientific and Cultural Organization.

Article 21

This Convention shall enter into force three months after the date of the deposit of the third instrument of ratification, acceptance or accession, but only with respect to those States which have deposited their respective instruments on or before that date. It shall enter into force with respect to any other State three months after the deposit of its instrument of ratification, acceptance or accession.

Article 22

The States Parties to this Convention recognize that the Convention is applicable not only to their metropolitan territories but also to all territories for the international relations of which they are responsible; they undertake to consult, if necessary, the governments or other competent authorities of these territories on or before ratification, acceptance or accession with a view to securing the application of the Convention to those territories, and to notify the Director-General of the United Nations Educational, Scientific and Cultural Organization of the territories to which it is applied, the notification to take effect three months after the date of its receipt.

Article 23

1. Each State Party to this Convention may denounce the Convention on its own behalf or on behalf of any territory for whose international relations it is responsible.

2. The denunciation shall be notified by an instrument in writing, deposited with the Director-General of the United Nations Educational, Scientific and Cultural Organiztion.

3. The denunciation shall take effect twelve months after the receipt of the instrument of denunciation.

Article 24

The Director-General of the United Nations Educational, Scientific and Cultural Organization shall inform the States members of the Organization, the States not members of the Organization which are referred to in Article 20, as well as the United Nations, of the deposit of all the instruments of ratification, acceptance and accession provided for in Articles 19 and 20, and of the notifications and denunciations provided for in Articles 22 and 23 respectively.

Article 25

1. This Convention may be revised by the General Conference of the United Nations Educational, Scientific and Cultural Organization. Any such revision

shall, however, bind only the States which shall become Parties to the revising convention.

2. If the General Conference should adopt a new convention revising this Convention in whole or in part, then, unless the new convention otherwise provides, this Convention shall cease to be open to ratification, acceptance or accession, as from the date on which the new revising convention enters into force.

Article 26

In conformity with Article 102 of the Charter of the United Nations, this Convention shall be registered with the Secretariat of the United Nations at the request of the Director-General of the United Nations Educational, Scientific and Cultural Organization.

Done in Paris this seventeenth day of November 1970, in two authentic copies bearing the signature of the President of the sixteenth session of the General Conference and of the Director-General of the United Nations Educational, Scientific and Cultural Organization, which shall be deposited in the archives of the United Nations Educational, Scientific and Cultural Organization, and certified true copies of which shall be delivered to all the States referred to in Articles 19 and 20 as well as to the United Nations.

The foregoing is the authentic text of the Convention duly adopted by the General Conference of the United Nations Educational, Scientific and Cultural Organization during its sixteenth session, which was held in Paris and declared closed the fourteenth day of November 1970.

IN FAITH WHEREOF we have appended our signatures this seventeenth day of November 1970.

The President of the General Conference   *The Director-General*

State of ratifications (R), acceptances (A) and accessions (a) as at 31 October 1984

Depositary: Unesco
Entry into force: 24 April 1972, in accordance with Article 21
Authoritative texts: English, French, Russian, Spanish
Registration at the Secretariat of the United Nations: 9 May 1972, No. 11806

	Date of deposit of instrument
Algeria	24 June 1974 R
Argentina	11 January 1973 R
Bolivia	4 October 1976 R
Brazil	16 February 1973 R
Bulgaria	15 September 1971 R
Cameroon	24 May 1972 R
Canada	28 March 1978 A
Central African Republic	1 February 1972 R
Cuba	30 January 1980 R
Cyprus	19 October 1979 R
Czechoslovakia	14 February 1977 A
Democratic Kampuchea	26 September 1972 R
Democratic People's Republic of Korea	13 May 1983 R
Dominican Republic	7 March 1973 R
Ecuador	24 March 1971 A
Egypt	5 April 1973 A
El Salvador	20 February 1978 R
German Democratic Republic	16 January 1974 A
Greece	5 June 1981 R
Guinea	18 March 1979 R
Honduras	19 March 1979 R

IV.A.4.Ratif.

	Date of deposit of instrument
Hungary	23 October 1978 R
India	24 January 1977 R
Iran	27 January 1975 A
Iraq	12 February 1973 A
Italy	2 October 1978 R
Jordan	15 March 1974 R
Kuwait	22 June 1972 A
Libyan Arab Jamahiriya	9 January 1973 R
Mauritania	27 April 1977 R
Mauritius	27 February 1978 A
Mexico	4 October 1972 A
Nepal	23 June 1976 R
Nicaragua	19 April 1977 R
Niger	16 October 1972 R
Nigeria	24 January 1972 R
Oman	2 June 1978 A
Pakistan	30 April 1981 R
Panama	13 August 1973 A
Peru	24 October 1979 A
Poland	31 January 1974 R
Qatar	20 April 1977 A
Republic of Korea	14 February 1983 A
Saudi Arabia	8 September 1976 A
Sri Lanka	7 April 1981 A
Syrian Arab Republic	21 February 1975 A
Tunisia	10 March 1975 R
Turkey	21 April 1981 R
United Republic of Tanzania	2 August 1977 R
United States of America	2 September 1983 A
Uruguay	9 August 1977 R
Yugoslavia	3 October 1972 R
Zaire	23 September 1974 R

Declarations and reservations

Cuba
(Translation) 'The Government of the Republic of Cuba considers that the implementation of the provisions contained in Articles 22 and 23 of the Convention is contrary to the Declaration on Granting Independence to Colonial Countries and Peoples (Resolution 1514) adopted by the United Nations General Assembly on 14 December 1960, which proclaims the necessity of bringing to a speedy and unconditional end colonialization in all its forms and manifestations.' (See letter LA/Depositary/1980/7 of 11 March 1980.)

Czechoslovakia
'Accepting the Convention, the Government of the Czechoslovak Socialist Republic wishes to declare that preservation of the state of dependence of certain countries from which the provisions of Articles 12, 22 and 23 proceed is in contradiction with the contents and objective of the Declaration of the United Nations General Assembly (Resolution 1514) on the granting of independence to colonial countries and nations of 14 December 1960. The Government of the Czechoslovak Socialist Republic further declares in connection with Article 20 that the Convention, according to the problems it regulates, should be open also to non-Member States of the United Nations Educational, Scientific and Cultural Organization without the need of invitation by the Executive Council of the United Nations Educational, Scientific and Cultural Organization.' (See letter LA/Depositary/1977/6 of 8 April 1977.)

Hungary
'Articles 12, 22 and 23 of the Convention contradict United Nations General Assembly Resolution 1514(XV) of 14 December 1960, which proclaimed the necessity of bringing to a speedy and unconditional end colonialism in all its forms and manifestations. Article 20 of the Convention is not in conformity with the principle of the sovereign equality of States; in view of the matters it regulates, the Convention should be open to all States without restriction.' (See letter LA Depositary/1978/17 of 12 December 1978.)

IV.A.4.Ratif. 3

Convention concerning the Protection of the World Cultural and Natural Heritage[1]

Introduction

This Convention makes the past practice of the Organization regarding international co-operation for the protection of the cultural heritage of mankind generally applicable and, as it were, codifies it, and extends such co-operation to the natural heritage, whose protection is obviously all the more necessary in that pollution of the environment has grown considerably worse.

The items protected by the Convention are those pertaining to the cultural or natural heritage which are of outstanding universal value from the point of view of history, art, science or aesthetics.

The Convention lays down two basic principles. First, each State Party to the Convention recognizes that the duty of ensuring conservation of elements of the world heritage situated in its territory lies primarily with it, and undertakes to act to this end, to the utmost of its own resources. Secondly, all the Contracting States recognize that it is the duty of the international community as a whole to co-operate in ensuring the conservation of a heritage which is of universal character.

For this purpose, each State Party to the Convention is required to draw up an inventory of property forming part of the cultural and natural heritage which is situated in its territory and suitable for protection under the Convention. On the basis of these inventories, the World Heritage Committee designates the items which, being regarded as forming part of the world heritage, are to form the protective measures provided for by the Convention.

1. Adopted on 16 November 1972 by the General Conference of Unesco at its seventeenth session, held in Paris.

IV.A.5.Intro.1

A special fund, financed mainly from regular contributions from States Parties, enables international assistance to be given for the conservation of such property forming part of the world heritage.

The Convention came into force on 17 December 1975.

United Nations Educational, Scientific and
Cultural Organization

Convention concerning the Protection of the World Cultural and Natural Heritage

Adopted by the General Conference at its
seventeenth session, Paris, 16 November 1972

The General Conference of the United Nations Educational, Scientific and Cultural Organization meeting in Paris from 17 October to 21 November 1972, at its seventeenth session,

Noting that the cultural heritage and the natural heritage are increasingly threatened with destruction not only by the traditional causes of decay, but also by changing social and economic conditions which aggravate the situation with even more formidable phenomena of damage or destruction.

Considering that deterioration or disappearance of any item of the cultural or natural heritage constitutes a harmful impoverishment of the heritage of all the nations of the world,

Considering that protection of this heritage at the national level often remains incomplete because of the scale of the resources which it requires and of the insufficient economic, scientific and technical resources of the country where the property to be protected is situated,

Recalling that the Constitution of the Organization provides that it will maintain, increase and diffuse knowledge, by assuring the conservation and protection of the world's heritage, and recommending to the nations concerned the necessary international conventions,

Considering that the existing international conventions, recommendations and resolutions concerning cultural and natural property demonstrate the importance, for all the peoples of the world, of safeguarding this unique and irreplaceable property, to whatever people it may belong,

Considering that parts of the cultural or natural heritage are of outstanding interest and therefore need to be preserved as part of the world heritage of mankind as a whole,

Considering that, in view of the magnitude and gravity of the new dangers

IV.A.5

threatening them, it is incumbent on the international community as a whole to participate in the protection of the cultural and natural heritage of outstanding universal value, by the granting of collective assistance which, although not taking the place of action by the State concerned, will serve as an effective complement thereto,

Considering that it is essential for this purpose to adopt new provisions in the form of a convention establishing an effective system of collective protection of the cultural and natural heritage of outstanding universal value, organized on a permanent basis and in accordance with modern scientific methods,

Having decided, at its sixteenth session, that this question should be made the subject of an international convention,

Adopts this sixteenth day of November 1972 this Convention.

I. Definitions of the cultural and the natural heritage

Article 1

For the purposes of this Convention, the following shall be considered as 'cultural heritage':

monuments: architectural works, works of monumental sculpture and painting, elements or structures of an archaeological nature, inscriptions, cave dwellings and combinations of features, which are of outstanding universal value from the point of view of history, art or science;

groups of buildings: groups of separate or connected buildings which, because of their architecture, their homogeneity or their place in the landscape, are of outstanding universal value from the point of view of history, art or science;

sites: works of man or the combined works of nature and of man, and areas including archaeological sites which are of outstanding universal value from the historical, aesthetic, ethnological or anthropological points of view.

Article 2

For the purposes of this Convention, the following shall be considered as 'natural heritage':

natural features consisting of physical and biological formations or groups of such formations, which are of outstanding universal value from the aesthetic or scientific point of view;

geological and physiographical formations and precisely delineated areas which constitute the habitat of threatened species of animals and plants of outstanding universal value from the point of view of science or conservation;

natural sites or precisely delineated natural areas of outstanding universal value from the point of view of science, conservation or natural beauty.

Article 3

It is for each State Party to this Convention to identify and delineate the different properties situated on its territory mentioned in Articles 1 and 2 above.

II. National protection and international protection of the cultural and natural heritage

Article 4

Each State Party to this Convention recognizes that the duty of ensuring the identification, protection, conservation, presentation and transmission to future generations of the cultural and natural heritage referred to in Articles 1 and 2 and situated on its territory, belongs primarily to that State. It will do all it can to this end, to the utmost of its own resources and, where appropriate, with any international assistance and co-operation, in particular, financial, artistic, scientific and technical, which it may be able to obtain.

Article 5

To ensure that effective and active measures are taken for the protection, conservation and presentation of the cultural and natural heritage situated on its territory, each State Party to this Convention shall endeavour, in so far as possible, and as appropriate for each country:

(a) to adopt a general policy which aims to give the cultural and natural heritage a function in the life of the community and to integrate the protection of that heritage into comprehensive planning programmes;

(b) to set up within its territories, where such services do not exist, one or more services for the protection, conservation and presentation of the cultural and natural heritage with an appropriate staff and possessing the means to discharge their functions;

(c) to develop scientific and technical studies and research and to work out such operating methods as will make the State capable of counteracting the dangers that threaten its cultural or natural heritage;

(d) to take the appropriate legal, scientific, technical, administrative and financial measures necessary for the identification, protection, conservation, presentation and rehabilitation of this heritage; and

(e) to foster the establishment or development of national or regional centres for training in the protection, conservation and presentation of the cultural and natural heritage and to encourage scientific research in this field.

Article 6

1. Whilst fully respecting the sovereignty of the States on whose territory the cultural and natural heritage mentioned in Articles 1 and 2 is situated; and without prejudice to property rights provided by national legislation, the States Parties to this Convention recognize that such heritage constitutes a world heritage for whose protection it is the duty of the international community as a whole to co-operate.

2. The States Parties undertake, in accordance with the provisions of this Convention, to give their help in the identification, protection, conservation and preservation of the cultural and natural heritage referred to in paragraphs 2 and 4 of Article 11 if the States on whose territory it is situated so request.

3. Each State Party to this Convention undertakes not to take any deliberate measures which might damage directly or indirectly the cultural and natural heritage referred to in Articles 1 and 2 situated on the territory of other States Parties to this Convention.

Article 7

For the purpose of this Convention, international protection of the world cultural and natural heritage shall be understood to mean the establishment of a system of international co-operation and assistance designed to support States Parties to the Convention in their efforts to conserve and identify that heritage.

III. Intergovernmental Committee for the Protection of the World Cultural and Natural Heritage

Article 8

1. An Intergovernmental Committee for the Protection of the Cultural and Natural Heritage of Outstanding Universal Value, called 'the World Heritage Committee', is hereby established within the United Nations Educational, Scientific and Cultural Organization. It shall be composed of 15 States Parties to the Convention, elected by States Parties to the Convention meeting in

general assembly during the ordinary session of the General Conference of the United Nations Educational, Scientific and Cultural Organization. The number of States members of the Committee shall be increased to 21 as from the date of the ordinary session of the General Conference following the entry into force of this Convention for at least 40 States.

2. Election of members of the Committee shall ensure an equitable representation of the different regions and cultures of the world.

3. A representative of the International Centre for the Study of the Preservation and Restoration of Cultural Property (Rome Centre), a representative of the International Council of Monuments and Sites (ICOMOS) and a representative of the International Union for Conservation of Nature and Natural Resources (IUCN), to whom may be added, at the request of States Parties to the Convention meeting in general assembly during the ordinary sessions of the General Conference of the United Nations Educational, Scientific and Cultural Organization, representatives of other intergovernmental or non-governmental organizations, with similar objectives, may attend the meetings of the Committee in an advisory capacity.

Article 9

1. The term of office of States members of the World Heritage Committee shall extend from the end of the ordinary session of the General Conference during which they are elected until the end of its third subsequent ordinary session.

2. The term of office of one-third of the members designated at the time of the first election shall, however, cease at the end of the first ordinary session of the General Conference following that at which they were elected; and the term of office of a further third of the members designated at the same time shall cease at the end of the second ordinary session of the General Conference following that at which they were elected. The names of these members shall be chosen by lot by the President of the General Conference of the United Nations Educational, Scientific and Cultural Organization after the first election.

3. States members of the Committee shall choose as their representatives persons qualified in the field of the cultural or natural heritage.

Article 10

1. The World Heritage Committee shall adopt its Rules of Procedure.

IV.A.5

2. The Committee may at any time invite public or private organizations or individuals to participate in its meetings for consultation on particular problems.

Article 11

1. Every State Party to this Convention shall, in so far as possible, submit to the World Heritage Committee an inventory of property forming part of the cultural and natural heritage, situated in its territory and suitable for inclusion in the list provided for in paragraph 2 of this Article. This inventory, which shall not be considered exhaustive, shall include documentation about the location of the property in question and its significance.

2. On the basis of the inventories submitted by States in accordance with paragraph 1, the Committee shall establish, keep up to date and publish, under the title of *World Heritage List*, a list of properties forming part of the cultural heritage and natural heritage, as defined in Articles 1 and 2 of this Convention, which it considers as having outstanding universal value in terms of such criteria as it shall have established. An updated list shall be distributed at least every two years.

3. The inclusion of a property in the *World Heritage List* requires the consent of the State concerned. The inclusion of a property situated in a territory, sovereignty or jurisdiction over which is claimed by more than one State shall in no way prejudice the rights of the parties to the dispute.

4. The Committee shall establish, keep up to date and publish, whenever circumstances shall so require, under the title of *List of World Heritage in Danger*, a list of the property appearing in the *World Heritage List* for the conservation of which major operations are necessary and for which assistance has been requested under this Convention. This list shall contain an estimate of the cost of such operations. The list may include only such property forming part of the cultural and natural heritage as is threatened by serious and specific dangers, such as the threat of disappearance caused by accelerated deterioration, large-scale public or private projects or rapid urban or tourist development projects; destruction caused by changes in the use or ownership of the land; major alterations due to unknown causes; abandonment for any reason whatsoever; the outbreak or the threat of an armed conflict; calamities and cataclysms; serious fires, earthquakes, landslides; volcanic eruptions; changes in water level, floods, and tidal waves. The Committee may at any time, in case of urgent need, make a new entry in the *List of World Heritage in Danger* and publicize such entry immediately.

5. The Committee shall define the criteria on the basis of which a property belonging to the cultural or natural heritage may be included in either of the lists mentioned in paragraphs 2 and 4 of this article.

6. Before refusing a request for inclusion in one of the two lists mentioned in paragraphs 2 and 4 of this article, the Committee shall consult the State Party in whose territory the cultural or natural property in question is situated.

7. The Committee shall, with the agreement of the States concerned, co-ordinate and encourage the studies and research needed for the drawing up of the lists referred to in paragraphs 2 and 4 of this article.

Article 12

The fact that a property belonging to the cultural or natural heritage has not been included in either of the two lists mentioned in paragraphs 2 and 4 of Article 11 shall in no way be construed to mean that it does not have an outstanding universal value for purposes other than those resulting from inclusion in these lists.

Article 13

1. The World Heritage Committee shall receive and study requests for international assistance formulated by States Parties to this Convention with respect to property forming part of the cultural or natural heritage, situated in their territories, and included or potentially suitable for inclusion in the lists referred to in paragraphs 2 and 4 of Article 11. The purpose of such requests may be to secure the protection, conservation, presentation or rehabilitation of such property.

2. Requests for international assistance under paragraph 1 of this article may also be concerned with identification of cultural or natural property defined in Articles 1 and 2, when preliminary investigations have shown that further inquiries would be justified.

3. The Committee shall decide on the action to be taken with regard to these requests, determine where appropriate, the nature and extent of its assistance, and authorize the conclusion, on its behalf, of the necessary arrangements with the government concerned.

4. The Committee shall determine an order of priorities for its operations. It shall in so doing bear in mind the respective importance for the world cultural and natural heritage of the property requiring protection, the need to give

IV.A.5

international assistance to the property most representative of a natural environment or of the genius and the history of the peoples of the world, the urgency of the work to be done, the resources available to the States on whose territory the threatenened property is situated and in particular the extent to which they are able to safeguard such property by their own means.

5. The Committee shall draw up, keep up to date and publicize a list of property for which international assistance has been granted.

6. The Committee shall decide on the use of the resources of the Fund established under Article 15 of this Convention. It shall seek ways of increasing these resources and shall take all useful steps to this end.

7. The Committee shall co-operate with international and national governmental and non-governmental organizations having objectives similar to those of this Convention. For the implementation of its programmes and projects, the Committee may call on such organizations, particularly the International Centre for the Study of the Preservation and Restoration of Cultural Property (the Rome Centre), the International Council of Monuments and Sites (ICOMOS) and the International Union for Conservation of Nature and Natural Resources (IUCN), as well as on public and private bodies and individuals.

8. Decisions of the Committee shall be taken by a majority of two-thirds of its members present and voting. A majority of the members of the Committee shall constitute a quorum.

Article 14

1. The World Heritage Committee shall be assisted by a Secretariat appointed by the Director-General of the United Nations Educational, Scientific and Cultural Organization.

2. The Director-General of the United Nations Educational, Scientific and Cultural Organization, utilizing to the fullest extent possible the services of the International Centre for the Study of the Preservation and the Restoration of Cultural Property (the Rome Centre), the International Council of Monuments and Sites (ICOMOS) and the International Union for Conservation of Nature and Natural Resources (IUCN) in their respective areas of competence and capability, shall prepare the Committee's documentation and the agenda of its meetings and shall have the responsibility for the implementation of its decisions.

IV. Fund for the Protection of the World Cultural and Natural Heritage

Article 15

1. A Fund for the Protection of the World Cultural and Natural Heritage of Outstanding Universal Value, called 'the World Heritage Fund', is hereby established.

2. The Fund shall constitute a trust fund, in conformity with the provisions of the Financial Regulations of the United Nations Educational, Scientific and Cultural Organization.

3. The resources of the Fund shall consist of:
(a) compulsory and voluntary contributions made by the States Parties to this Convention,
(b) contributions, gifts or bequests which may be made by:
   (i) other States;
   (ii) the United Nations Educational, Scientific and Cultural Organization, other organizations of the United Nations system, particularly the United Nations Development Programme or other intergovernmental organizations;
   (iii) public or private bodies or individuals;
(c) any interest due on the resources of the Fund;
(d) funds raised by collections and receipts from events organized for the benefit of the Fund; and
(e) all other resources authorized by the Fund's regulations, as drawn up by the World Heritage Committee.

4. Contributions to the Fund and other forms of assistance made available to the Committee may be used only for such purposes as the Committee shall define. The Committee may accept contributions to be used only for a certain programme or project, provided that the Committee shall have decided on the implementation of such programme or project. No political conditions may be attached to contributions made to the Fund.

Article 16

1. Without prejudice to any supplementary voluntary contribution, the States Parties to this Convention undertake to pay regularly, every two years, to the World Heritage Fund, contributions, the amount of which, in the form of a uniform percentage applicable to all States, shall be determined by the Gen-

eral Assembly of States Parties to the Convention, meeting during the sessions of the General Conference of the United Nations Educational, Scientific and Cultural Organization. This decision of the General Assembly requires the majority of the States Parties present and voting, which have not made the declaration referred to in paragraph 2 of this Article. In no case shall the compulsory contribution of States Parties to the Convention exceed 1% of the contribution to the Regular Budget of the United Nations Educational, Scientific and Cultural Organization.

2.   However, each State referred to in Article 31 or in Article 32 of this Convention may declare, at the time of the deposit of its instruments of ratification, acceptance or accession, that it shall not be bound by the provisions of paragraph 1 of this Article.

3.   A State Party to the Convention which has made the declaration referred to in paragraph 2 of this Article may at any time withdraw the said declaration by notifying the Director-General of the United Nations Educational, Scientific and Cultural Organization. However, the withdrawal of the declaration shall not take effect in regard to the compulsory contribution due by the State until the date of the subsequent General Assembly of States Parties to the Convention.

4.   In order that the Committee may be able to plan its operations effectively, the contributions of States Parties to this Convention which have made the declaration referred to in paragraph 2 of this Article, shall be paid on a regular basis, at least every two years, and should not be less than the contributions which they should have paid if they had been bound by the provisions of paragraph 1 of this Article.

5.   Any State Party to the Convention which is in arrears with the payment of its compulsory or voluntary contribution for the current year and the calendar year immediately preceding it shall not be eligible as a Member of the World Heritage Committee, although this provision shall not apply to the first election.

The terms of office of any such State which is already a member of the Committee shall terminate at the time of the elections provided for in Article 8, paragraph 1 of this Convention.

Article 17

The States Parties to this Convention shall consider or encourage the establishment of national, public and private foundations or associations whose purpose is to invite donations for the protection of the cultural and natural heritage as defined in Articles 1 and 2 of this Convention.

Article 18

The States Parties to this Convention shall give their assistance to international fund-raising campaigns organized for the World Heritage Fund under the auspices of the United Nations Educational, Scientific and Cultural Organization. They shall facilitate collections made by the bodies mentioned in paragraph 3 of Article 15 for this purpose.

V. Conditions and arrangements for international assistance

Article 19

Any State Party to this Convention may request international assistance for property forming part of the cultural or natural heritage of outstanding universal value situated within its territory. It shall submit with its request such information and documentation provided for in Article 21 as it has in its possession and as will enable the Committee to come to a decision.

Article 20

Subject to the provisions of paragraph 2 of Article 13, sub-paragraph (c) of Article 22 and Article 23, international assistance provided for by this Convention may be granted only to property forming part of the cultural and natural heritage which the World Heritage Committee has decided, or may decide, to enter in one of the lists mentioned in paragraphs 2 and 4 of Article 11.

Article 21

1. The World Heritage Committee shall define the procedure by which requests to it for international assistance shall be considered and shall specify the content of the request, which should define the operation contemplated, the work that is necessary, the expected cost thereof, the degree of urgency and the reasons why the resources of the State requesting assistance do not allow it to meet all the expenses. Such requests must be supported by experts' reports whenever possible.

2. Requests based upon disasters or natural calamities should, by reasons of the urgent work which they may involve, be given immediate, priority consideration by the Committee, which should have a reserve fund at its disposal against such contingencies.

3. Before coming to a decision, the Committee shall carry out such studies and consultations as it deems necessary.

Article 22

Assistance granted by the World Heritage Committee may take the following forms:

(a) studies concerning the artistic, scientific and technical problems raised by the protection, conservation, presentation and rehabilitation of the cultural and natural heritage, as defined in paragraphs 2 and 4 of Article 11 of this Convention; ˙

(b) provision of experts, technicians and skilled labour to ensure that the approved work is correctly carried out;

(c) training of staff and specialists at all levels in the field of identification, protection, conservation, presentation and rehabilitation of the cultural and natural heritage;

(d) supply of equipment which the State concerned does not possess or is not in a position to acquire;

(e) low-interest or interest-free loans which might be repayable on a long-term basis;

(f) the granting, in exceptional cases and for special reasons, of non-repayable subsidies.

Article 23

The World Heritage Committee may also provide international assistance to national or regional centres for the training of staff and specialists at all levels in the field of identification, protection, conservation, presentation and rehabilitation of the cultural and natural heritage.

Article 24

International assistance on a large scale shall be preceded by detailed scientific, economic and technical studies. These studies shall draw upon the most advanced techniques for the protection, conservation, presentation and rehabilitation of the natural and cultural heritage and shall be consistent with the objectives of this Convention. The studies shall also seek means of making rational use of the resources available in the State concerned.

IV.A.5

Article 25

As a general rule, only part of the cost of work necessary shall be borne by the international community. The contribution of the State benefiting from international assistance shall constitute a substantial share of the resources devoted to each programme or project, unless its resources do not permit this.

Article 26

The World Heritage Committee and the recipient State shall define in the agreement they conclude the conditions in which a programme or project for which international assistance under the terms of this Convention is provided, shall be carried out. It shall be the responsibility of the State receiving such international assistance to continue to protect, conserve and present the property so safeguarded, in observance of the conditions laid down by the agreement.

VI. Educational programmes

Article 27

1. The States Parties to this Convention shall endeavour by all appropriate means, and in particular by educational and information programmes, to strengthen appreciation and respect by their peoples of the cultural and natural heritage defined in Article 1 and 2 of the Convention.

2. They shall undertake to keep the public broadly informed of the dangers threatening this heritage and of activities carried on in pursuance of this Convention.

Article 28

States Parties to this Convention which receive international assistance under the Convention shall take appropriate measures to make known the importance of the property for which assistance has been received and the rôle played by such assistance.

VII. Reports

Article 29

1. The States Parties to this Convention shall, in the reports which they submit to the General Conference of the United Nations Educational, Scientific

and Cultural Organization on dates and in a manner to be determined by it, give information on the legislative and administrative provisions which they have adopted and other action which they have taken for the application of this Convention, together with details of the experience acquired in this field.

2. These reports shall be brought to the attention of the World Heritage Committee.

3. The Committee shall submit a report on its activities at each of the ordinary sessions of the General Conference of the United Nations Educational, Scientific and Cultural Organization.

VIII. Final clauses

Article 30

This Convention is drawn up in Arabic, English, French, Russian and Spanish, the five texts being equally authoritative.

Article 31

1. This Convention shall be subject to ratification or acceptance by States members of the United Nations Educational, Scientific and Cultural Organization in accordance with their respective constitutional procedures.

2. The instruments of ratification or acceptance shall be deposited with the Director-General of the United Nations Educational, Scientific and Cultural Organization.

Article 32

1. This Convention shall be open to accession by all States not members of the United Nations Educational, Scientific and Cultural Organization which are invited by the General Conference of the Organization to accede to it.

2. Accession shall be effected by the deposit of an instrument of accession with the Director-General of the United Nations Educational, Scientific and Cultural Organization.

Article 33

This Convention shall enter into force three months after the date of the deposit of the twentieth instrument of ratification, acceptance or accession, but only with respect to those States which have deposited their respective instruments of ratification, acceptance or accession on or before that date. It shall enter into force with respect to any other State three months after the deposit of its instrument of ratification, acceptance or accession.

Article 34

The following provisions shall apply to those States Parties to this Convention which have a federal or non-unitary constitutional system:
(a) with regard to the provisions of this Convention, the implementation of which comes under the legal jurisdiction of the federal or central legislative power, the obligations of the federal or central government shall be the same as for those States Parties which are not federal States;
(b) with regard to the provisions of this Convention, the implementation of which comes under the legal jurisdiction of individual constituent States, countries, provinces or cantons that are not obliged by the constitutional system of the federation to take legislative measures, the federal government shall inform the competent authorities of such States, countries, provinces or cantons of the said provisions, with its recommendation for their adoption.

Article 35

1. Each State Party to this Convention may denounce the Convention.

2. The denunciation shall be notified by an instrument in writing, deposited with the Director-General of the United Nations Educational, Scientific and Cultural Organization.

3. The denunciation shall take effect twelve months after the receipt of the instrument of denunciation. It shall not affect the financial obligations of the denouncing State until the date on which the withdrawal takes effect.

Article 36

The Director-General of the United Nations Educational, Scientific and Cultural Organization shall inform the States members of the Organization, the States not members of the Organization which are referred to in Article 32, as well as the United Nations, of the deposit of all the instruments of ratification, acceptance, or accession provided for in Articles 31 and 32, and of the denunciations provided for in Article 35.

Article 37

1. This Convention may be revised by the General Conference of the United Nations Educational, Scientific and Cultural Organization. Any such revision shall, however, bind only the States which shall become Parties to the revising convention.

2. If the General Conference should adopt a new convention revising this Convention in whole or in part, then, unless the new convention otherwise provides, this Convention shall cease to be open to ratification, acceptance or accession, as from the date on which the new revising convention enters into force.

Article 38

In conformity with Article 102 of the Charter of the United Nations, this Convention shall be registered with the Secretariat of the United Nations at the request of the Director-General of the United Nations Educational, Scientific and Cultural Organization.

Done in Paris, this twenty-third day of November 1972, in two authentic copies bearing the signature of the President of the seventeenth session of the General Conference and of the Director-General of the United Nations Educational, Scientific and Cultural Organization, and certified true copies of which shall be delivered to all the States referred to in Articles 31 and 32 as well as to the United Nations.

The foregoing is the authentic text of the Recommendation duly adopted by the General Conference of the United Nations Educational, Scientific and Cultural Organization during its seventeenth session, which was held in Paris and declared closed on the twenty-first day of November 1972.

IN FAITH WHEREOF we have appended our signatures this twenty-third day of November 1972.

The President of the General Conference   *The Director-General*

State of ratifications (R), acceptances (A) and accessions (a) as at 31 October 1984

Depository: Unesco
Entry into force: 17 December 1975, in accordance with Article 33
Authoritative tests: Arabic, English, French, Russian, Spanish
Registration at the Secretariat of the United Nations:
15 March 1977, No. 15511

	Date of deposit of instrument
Afghanistan	20 March 1979 R
Algeria	24 June 1974 R
Antigua and Barbuda	1 November 1983 A
Argentina	23 August 1978 A
Australia	22 August 1974 R
Bangladesh	3 August 1983 A
Benin	14 June 1982 R
Bolivia	4 October 1976 R
Brazil	1 September 1977 A[1]
Bulgaria	7 March 1974 A[1]
Burundi	19 May 1982 R
Cameroon	7 December 1982 R
Canada	23 July 1976 A
Central African Republic	22 December 1980 R
Chile	20 February 1980 R
Colombia	24 May 1983 A
Costa Rica	23 August 1977 R
Cuba	24 March 1981 R
Cyprus	14 August 1975 A
Democratic Yemen	7 October 1980 A
Denmark	25 July 1979 R[1]
Ecuador	16 June 1975 A
Egypt	7 February 1974 R

	Date of deposit of instrument
Ethiopia	6 July 1977 R
France	27 June 1975 A[1]
Germany, Federal Republic of	23 August 1976 R[1,2]
Ghana	4 July 1975 R
Greece	17 July 1981 R
Guatemala	16 January 1979 R
Guinea	18 March 1979 R
Guyana	20 June 1977 A
Haiti	18 January 1980 R
Holy See	7 October 1982 a
Honduras	8 June 1979 R
India	14 November 1977 R
Iran, Islamic Republic of	26 February 1975 A
Iraq	5 March 1974 A
Italy	23 June 1978 R
Ivory Coast	9 January 1981 R
Jamaica	14 June 1983 A
Jordan	5 May 1975 R
Lebanon	3 February 1983 R
Libyan Arab Jamahiriya	13 October 1978 R
Luxembourg	28 September 1983 R
Madagascar	19 July 1983 R
Malawi	5 January 1982 R
Mali	5 April 1977 A
Malta	14 November 1978 A
Mauritania	2 March 1981 R
Mexico	23 February 1984 A
Monaco	7 November 1978 R
Morocco	28 October 1975 R
Mozambique	27 November 1982 R
Nepal	20 June 1978 A
Nicaragua	17 December 1979 A
Niger	23 December 1974 A
Nigeria	23 October 1974 R
Norway	12 May 1977 R[1]
Oman	6 October 1981 A
Pakistan	23 July 1976 R
Panama	3 March 1978 R
Peru	24 February 1982 R
Poland	29 June 1976 R

Portugal	30 September 1980 R
Qatar	12 September 1984 A
Saudi Arabia	7 August 1978 A
Senegal	13 February 1976 R
Seychelles	9 April 1980 A
Spain	4 May 1982 A
Sri Lanka	6 June 1980 A
Sudan	6 June 1974 R
Switzerland	17 September 1975 R
Syrian Arab Republic	13 August 1975 A
Tunisia	10 March 1975 R
Turkey	16 March 1983 R
United Kingdom of Great Britain and Northern Ireland	29 May 1984 R
United Republic of Tanzania	2 August 1977 R
United States of America	7 December 1973 R[1]
Yemen	25 January 1984 R
Yugoslavia	26 May 1975 R
Zaire	23 September 1974 R
Zambia	4 June 1984 R
Zimbabwe	16 August 1982 R

Notes

1. With declaration made by virtue of Article 16, paragraph 2 of the Convention, according to which this State shall not be bound by the provisions of Article 16, paragraph 1 (see letters LA/Depositary/1976/27 of 9 October 1976, LA/Depositary/1977/26 of 7 December 1977, CL/2367 of 17 May 1974, LA/Depositary/1979/18 of 4 September 1979, CL/2345 Add. of 9 April 1974, CL/2473 of 9 September 1975 and LA/Depositary/1977/14 of 12 August 1977 respectively).

2. With declaration in terms of which the Convention (translation): 'shall also apply to Berlin (West) with effect from the date on which it shall enter into force for the Federal Republic of Germany' (see letter LA/Depositary/1976/27 of 9 October 1976).
   With regard to that notification, the Government of the Soviet Union declared (translation): 'In the view of the Soviet Authorities, it is possible only to take note of the declaration by which the Government of the Federal Republic of Germany extended to Berlin (West) the application of the Convention concerning the protection of the world cultural and natural heritage of 16 November 1972, it being understood that this extension shall be done in accordance with the provisions of the Quadripartite Agreement of 3 September 1971, in the respect of the established procedures.' (See letter LA/Depositary/1977 of 6 April 1977.)

IV.A.5.Ratif.

Declarations and reservations

Iraq
(Translation) 'Entry into the above Convention by the Republic of Iraq shall, however, in no way signify recognition of Israel or be conducive to entry into relations with it.' (See letter CL/2367 of 17 May 1974.)

Syrian Arab Republic
'1.   (Translation) The accession of the Syrian Arab Republic to the Convention adopted by the General Conference of Unesco at its seventeenth session on 16 November 1972 and its ratification by the Syrian Arab Government do not mean in any way its recognition of Israel and cannot result in the establishment of a direct contact with it that might be stipulated by the said Convention.
'2.   The Government of the Syrian Arab Republic views that the obligation emanated in Article 4 covers the occupied Arab territories and consequently, the Israeli occupation authorities are under obligation to preserve the cultural and natural heritage existing in the occupied territories in view of the fact that occupation does not eliminate sovreignty and that the occupation authorities are considered internationally responsible for any attenuation of the cultural and natural heritage even if Israel has not acceded to the Convention.
'3.   The Government of the Syrian Arab Republic views that paragraph 3 of Article 6 binds in its obligations therein contained the authorities occupying territories by force.
'4.   The Government of the Syrian Arab Republic views that the international co-operation system stipulated in Article 7 binds the Member States to exert all possible aid to the State whose part of its territories is occupied for the sake of preserving the natural and cultural heritage in the occupied territories against the aggressions of the occupying authorities.' (See letter CL/2491 of 23 October 1975.)

B. Recommendations

Recommendation on International Principles Applicable to Archeological Excavations[1]

Introduction

The protection of remains of the past lying beneath the ground or under water presents many problems, which are all the more difficult to solve internationally in that the interests of States may clash, especially as regards the appropriation of archaeological property.

The Recommendation provides that each State should make archaeological explorations subject to a system of supervision. It defines the conditions in which an authority to excavate may be granted, together with the obligations and rights of the excavator.

Chance finds of archaeological remains are to be declared as soon as possible.

With regard to the thorny question of the assignment of finds, the Recommendation establishes the principle that objects discovered should be used, in the first place, for building up museum collections in the country in which excavations are carried out. The return to the national or foreign excavator of copies or duplicates should be subject to the condition that they be allocated within a specified period of time to scientific centres open to the public.

In the event of armed conflict any State occupying the territory of another State should refrain from carrying out excavations in the occupied territory.

The Recommendation further advocates regulations to govern the trade in antiquities.

---

1. Adopted on 5 December 1956 by the General Conference of Unesco at its eighth session, held in New Delhi.

IV.B.1. Intro.

United Nations Educational, Scientific and
Cultural Organization

Recommendation on International Principles
Applicable to Archaeological Excavations

Adopted by the General Conference at its
ninth session, New Delhi, 5 December 1956

The General Conference of the United Nations Educational, Scientific and Cultural Organization, meeting at New Delhi, from 5 November to 5 December 1956, at its ninth session,

Being of the opinion that the surest guarantee for the preservation of monuments and works of the past rests in the respect and affection felt for them by the peoples themselves, and persuaded that such feelings may be greatly strengthened by adequate measures inspired by the wish of Member States to develop science and international relations,

Convinced that the feelings aroused by the contemplation and study of works of the past do much to foster mutual understanding between nations, and that it is therefore highly desirable to secure international co-operation with regard to them and to further, in every possible way, the fulfilment of their social mission,

Considering that, while individual States are more directly concerned with the archaeological discoveries made on their territory, the international community as a whole is nevertheless the richer for such discoveries,

Considering that the history of man implies the knowledge of all different civilizations; and that it is therefore necessary, in the general interest, that all archaeological remains be studied and, where possible, preserved and taken into safe keeping,

Convinced that it is highly desirable that the national authorities responsible for the protection of the archaeological heritage should be guided by certain common principles which have been tested by experience and put into practice by national archaeological services,

Being of the opinion that, though the regulation of excavations is first and foremost for the domestic jurisdiction of each State, this principle should be brought into harmony with that of a liberally understood and freely accepted international co-operation,

Having before it proposals concerning international principles applicable to archaeological excavations, which constitute item 9.4.3 on the agenda of the session,

Having decided, at its eighth session, that these proposals should be regulated at the international level by way of a recommendation to Member States,

Adopts, this fifth day of December 1956, the following Recommendation:

The General Conference recommends that Member States should apply the following provisions by taking whatever legislative or other steps may be required to give effect, within their respective territories, to the principles and norms formulated in the present Recommendation.

The General Conference recommends that Member States should bring the present Recommendation to the knowledge of authorities and organizations concerned with archaeological excavations and museums.

The General Conference recommends that Member States should report to it, on dates and in a manner to be determined by it, on the action which they have taken to give effect to the present Recommendation.

I. Definitions

Archaeological excavations

1. For the purpose of the present Recommendation, by archaeological excavations is meant any research aimed at the discovery of objects of archaeological character, whether such research involves digging of the ground or systematic exploration of its surface or is carried out on the bed or in the sub-soil of inland or territorial waters of a Member State.

Property protected

2. The provisions of the present Recommendation apply to any remains, whose preservation is in the public interest from the point of view of history or art and architecture, each Member State being free to adopt the most appropriate criterion for assessing the public interest of objects found on its territory. In particular, the provisions of the present Recommendation should apply to any monuments and movable or immovable objects of archaeological interest considered in the widest sense.

3. The criterion adopted for assessing the public interest of archaeological remains might vary according to whether it is a question of the preservation of such property, or of the excavator's or finder's obligation to declare his discoveries.

(a) In the former case, the criterion based on preserving all objects originating before a certain date should be abandoned, and replaced by one whereby protection is extended to all objects belonging to a given period or of a minimum age fixed by law.

(b) In the latter case, each Member State should adopt far wider criteria, compelling the excavator or finder to declare any object, of archaeological character, whether movable or immovable, which he may discover.

II. General principles

Protection of the archaeological heritage

4. Each Member State should ensure the protection of its archaeological heritage, taking fully into account problems arising in connexion with excavations, and in conformity with the provisions of the present Recommendation.

5. Each Member State should in particular:
(a) Make archaeological explorations and excavations subject to prior authorization by the competent authority;
(b) Oblige any person finding archaeological remains to declare them at the earliest possible date to the competent authority;
(c) Impose penalties for the infringement of these regulations;
(d) Make undeclared objects subject to confiscation;
(e) Define the legal status of the archaeological sub-soil and, where State ownership of the said sub-soil is recognized, specifically mention the fact in its legislation;
(f) Consider classifying as historical monuments the essential elements of its archaeological heritage.

Protecting body: archaeological excavations

6. Although differences of tradition and unequal financial resources make it impossible for all Member States to adopt a uniform system of organization in the administrative services responsible for excavations, certain common principles should nevertheless apply to all national archaeological services:
(a) The archaeological service should, so far as possible, be a central State administration—or at any rate an organization provided by law with the necessary means for carrying out any emergency measures that may ·be

required. In addition to the general administration of archaeological work, this service should co-operate with research institutes and universities in the technical training of excavators. This body should also set up a central documentation, including maps, of its movable and immovable monuments and additional documentation for every important museum or ceramic or iconographic collection, etc.

(b) Steps should be taken to ensure in particular the regular provision of funds: (i) to administer the services in a satisfactory manner; (ii) to carry out a programme of work proportionate to the archaeological resources of the country, including scientific publications; (iii) to exercise control over accidental discoveries; (iv) to provide for the upkeep of excavation sites and monuments.

7. Careful supervision should be exercised by each Member State over the restoration of archaeological remains and objects discovered.

8. Prior approval should be obtained from the competent authority for the removal of any monuments which ought to be preserved *in situ*.

9. Each Member State should consider maintaining untouched, partially or totally, a certain number of archaeological sites of different periods in order that their excavation may benefit from improved techniques and more advanced archaeological knowledge. On each of the larger sites now being excavated, in so far as the nature of the land permits, well defined 'witness' areas might be left unexcavated in several places in order to allow for eventual verification of the stratigraphy and archaeological composition of the site.

Formation of central and regional collections

10. Inasmuch as archaeology is a comparative science, account should be taken, in the setting up and organizing of museums and reserve collections, of the need for facilitating the work of comparison as much as possible. For this purpose, central and regional collections might be formed or, in exceptional cases, local collections on particularly important archaeological sites—in preference to small scattered collections, accessible to comparatively few people. These establishments should command, on a permanent basis, the administrative facilities and scientific staff necessary to ensure the preservation of the exhibits.

11. On important archaeological sites, a small exhibit of an educational nature—possibly a museum—should be set up to convey to visitors the interest of the archaeological remains.

Education of the public

12. The competent authority should initiate educational measures in order to arouse and develop respect and affection for the remains of the past by the teaching of history, the participation of students in certain excavations, the publication in the press of archaeological information supplied by recognized specialists, the organization of guided tours, exhibitions and lectures dealing with methods of excavation and results achieved, the clear display of archaeological sites explored and monuments discovered, and the publication of cheap and simply written monographs and guides. In order to encourage the public to visit these sites, Member States should make all necessary arrangements to facilitate access to them.

III. Regulations governing excavations and international collaboration

Authority to excavate granted to foreigners

13. Each Member State on whose territory excavations are to take place should lay down general rules governing the granting of excavation concessions, the conditions to be observed by the excavator, in particular as concerns the supervision exercised by the national authorities, the period of the concession, the reasons which may justify its withdrawal, the suspension of work, or its transfer from the authorized excavator to the national archaeological service.

14. The conditions imposed upon a foreign excavator should be those applicable to nationals. Consequently, the deed of concession should omit special stipulations which are not imperative.

International collaboration

15. In the higher interest of archaeology and of international collaboration, Member States should encourage excavations by a liberal policy. They might allow qualified individuals or learned bodies, irrespective of nationality, to apply on an equal footing for the concession to excavate. Member States should encourage excavations carried out by joint missions of scientists from their own country and of archaeologists representing foreign institutions, or by international missions.

IV.B.1

16. When a concession is granted to a foreign mission, the representative of the conceding State—if such be appointed—should, as far as possible, also be an archaeologist capable of helping the mission and collaborating with it.

17. Member States which lack the necessary resources for the organization of archaeological excavations in foreign countries should be accorded facilities for sending archaeologists to sites being worked by other Member States, with the consent of the director of excavations.

18. A Member State whose technical or other resources are insufficient for the scientific carrying out of an excavation should be able to call on the participation of foreign experts or on a foreign mission to undertake it.

Reciprocal guarantees

19. Authority to carry out excavations should be granted only to institutions represented by qualified archaeologists or to persons offering such unimpeachable scientific, moral and financial guarantees as to ensure that any excavations will be completed in accordance with the terms of the deed of concession and within the period laid down.

20. On the other hand, when authority to carry out excavations is granted to foreign archaeologists, it should guarantee them a period of work long enough, and conditions of security sufficient to facilitate their task and protect them from unjustified cancellation of the concession in the event, for instance, of their being obliged, for reasons recognized as valid, to interrupt their work for a given period of time.

Preservation of archaeological remains

21. The deed of concession should define the obligations of the excavator during and on completion of his work. The deed should, in particular, provide for guarding, maintenance and restoration of the site together with the conservation, during and on completion of his work, of objects and monuments uncovered. The deed should moreover indicate what help if any the excavator might expect from the conceding State in the discharge of his obligations should these prove too onerous.

Access to excavation sites

22. Qualified experts of any nationality should be allowed to visit a site before a report of the work is published and with the consent of the director of

excavations, even during the work. This privilege should in no case jeopardize the excavator's scientific rights in his finds.

Assignment of finds

23. (a) Each Member State should clearly define the principles which hold good on its territory in regard to the disposal of finds from excavations.

(b) Finds should be used, in the first place, for building up, in the museums of the country in which excavations are carried out, complete collections fully representative of that country's civilization, history, art and architecture.

(c) With the main object of promoting archaeological studies through the distribution of original material, the conceding authority, after scientific publication, might consider allocating to the approved excavator a number of finds from his excavation, consisting of duplicates or, in a more general sense, of objects or groups of objects which can be released in view of their similarity to other objects from the same excavation. The return to the excavator of objects resulting from excavations should always be subject to the condition that they be allocated within a specified period of time to scientific centres open to the public, with the proviso that if these conditions are not put into effect, or cease to be carried out, the released objects will be returned to the conceding authority.

(d) Temporary export of finds, excluding objects which are exceptionally fragile or of national importance, should be authorized on requests emanating from a scientific institution of public or private character if the study of these finds in the conceding State is not possible because of lack of bibliographical or scientific facilities, or is impeded by difficulties of access.

(e) Each Member State should consider ceding to, exchanging with, or depositing in foreign museums objects which are not required in the national collections.

Scientific rights; rights and obligations of the excavator

24. (a) The conceding State should guarantee to the excavator scientific rights in his finds for a reasonable period.

(b) The conceding State should require the excavator to publish the results of his work within the period stipulated in the deed, or, failing such stipulations, within a reasonable period. This period should not exceed two years for the preliminary report. For a period of five years following the discovery, the competent archaeological authorities should undertake not to release the complete collection of finds, nor the relative scientific documentation, for detailed study, without the written authority of the excavator. Subject to the same conditions, these authorities should also prevent photographic or other reproduction of archaeological material still unpublished. In order to allow, should it be so desired, for simultaneous publication of the preliminary report in both countries, the excavator should, on demand, submit a copy of his text to these authorities.

(c) Scientific publications dealing with archaeological research and issued in a language which is not widely used should include a summary and, if possible, a list of contents and captions of illustrations translated into some more widely known language.

Documentation on excavations

25. Subject to the provisions set out in paragraph 24, the national archaeological services should, as far as possible, make their documentation and reserve collections of archaeological material readily available for inspection and study to excavators and qualified experts, especially those who have been granted a concession for a particular site or who wish to obtain one.

Regional meetings and scientific discussions

26. In order to facilitate the study of problems of common interest, Member States might, from time to time, convene regional meetings attended by representatives of the archaeological services of interested States. Similarly, each Member State might encourage excavators working on its soil to meet for scientific discussions.

IV. Trade in antiquities

27. In the higher interests of the common archaeological heritage, each Member State should consider the adoption of regulations to govern the trade in antiquities so as to ensure that this trade does not encourage smuggling of archaeological material or affect adversely the protection of sites and the collecting of material for public exhibit.

28. Foreign museums should, in order to fulfil their scientific and educational aims, be able to acquire objects which have been released from any restrictions due to the laws in force in the country of origin.

V. Repression of clandestine excavations and of the illicit export of archaeological finds

Protection of archaeological sites against clandestine excavations and damage

29. Each Member State should take all necessary measures to prevent clandestine excavations and damage to monunents defined in paragraphs 2 and 3 above, and also to prevent the export of objects thus obtained.

International co-operation in repressive measures

30. All necessary measures should be taken in order that museums to which archaeological objects are offered ascertain that there is no reason to believe that these objects have been procured by clandestine excavation, theft or any other method regarded as illicit by the competent authorities of the country of origin. Any suspicious offer and all details appertaining thereto should be brought to the attention of the services concerned. When archaeological objects have been acquired by museums, adequate details allowing them to be identified and indicating the manner of their acquisition should be published as soon as possible.

Return of objects to their country of origin

31. Excavation services and museums should lend one another assistance in order to ensure or facilitate the recovery of objects derived from clandestine excavations or theft, and of all objects exported in infringement of the legislation of the country of origin. It is desirable that each Member State should take the necessary measures to ensure this recovery. These principles should be applied in the event of temporary exports as mentioned in paragraph 23(c), (d) and (e) above, if the objects are not returned within the stipulated period.

VI. Excavations in occupied territory

32. In the event of armed conflict, any Member State occupying the territory of another State should refrain from carrying out archaeological excavations in the occupied territory. In the event of chance finds being made, particularly during military works, the occupying Power should take all possible measures to protect these finds, which should be handed over, on the termination of hostilities, to the competent authorities of the territory previously occupied, together with all documentation relating thereto.

VII. Bilateral agreements

33. Member States should, whenever necessary or desirable, conclude bilateral agreements to deal with matters of common interest arising out of the application of the present Recommendation.

The foregoing is the authentic text of the Recommendation duly adopted by the General Conference of the United Nations Educational, Scientific and Cultural Organization during its Ninth Session, which was held at New Delhi and declared closed the fifth day of December 1956.

IN FAITH WHEREOF we have appended our signatures this fifth day of December 1956.

The President of the General Conference   *The Director-General*

Recommendation concerning the most Effective Means of Rendering Museums Accessible to Everyone[1]

Introduction

This Recommendation urges that, in order that museums may contribute to the education of the public through all stages of life, a permanent link should be established between museums, educational authorities, professional organizations, the social services of industrial and commercial enterprises, and the like.

The accessibility of museums to the public school entail not only the granting of material facilities, particularly with regard to admission charges and opening hours, but also the adoption of the necessary measures to ensure that collections are easy to appreciate.

The instrument further recommends that States do everything in their power to encourage people to visit museums and exhibitions.

---

1. Adopted on 14 December 1960 by the General Conference of Unesco at its eleventh session, held in Paris.

IV.B.2.Intro.

United Nations Educational, Scientific and
Cultural Organization

Recommendation concerning the most Effective Means of Rendering Museums Accessible to Everyone

Adopted by the General Conference at its
eleventh session, Paris, 14 December 1960

The General Conference of the United Nations Educational, Scientific and Cultural Organization, meeting in Paris from 14 November to 15 December 1960, at its eleventh session,

Considering that one of the functions of the Organization, as laid down in its Constitution, is to give fresh impulse to popular education and to the spread of culture, to collaborate in the work of advancing the mutual understanding of peoples by instituting collaboration among them to advance the ideal of equality of educational opportunity without regard to race, sex or any distinctions, economic or social, and to maintain, increase and diffuse knowledge,

Considering that museums can effectively contribute towards accomplishing these tasks,

Considering that museums of all kinds are a source of enjoyment and instruction,

Considering also that museums, by preserving works of art and scientific material and presenting them to the public, help to disseminate a knowledge of the various cultures and thus promote mutual understanding among nations,

Considering in consequence that every effort should be made to encourage all sections of the population, and especially the working classes, to visit museums,

Considering that with the progress in the industrial organization of the world, people have more leisure, and that such leisure should be used for the benefit and the cultural advancement of all,

Recognizing the new social conditions and needs which the museums must take into account in order to carry out their permanent educational mission and satisfy the cultural aspirations of the workers,

Having before it proposals concerning the most effective means of rendering museums accessible to everyone, constituting item 17.4.1 of the agenda of the session,

Having decided at its tenth session that proposals on the question should be the subject of international regulation by way of a recommendation to Member States,

Adopts this Recommendation on the fourteenth day of December 1960.

The General Conference recommends that Member States should apply the following provisions by taking whatever legislative or other steps may be required to give effect, within their respective territories, to the principles and norms set forth in this Recommendation.

The General Conference recommends that Member States should bring this Recommendation to the knowledge of the authorities and bodies concerned with museums, and of the museums themselves.

The General Conference recommends that Member States should report to it, on dates and in a manner to be determined by it, on the action they have taken to give effect to this Recommendation.

I. Definition

1. For the purposes of this Recommendation, the term 'museum' shall be taken to mean any permanent establishment administered in the general interest for the purpose of preserving, studying, enhancing by various means and, in particular, exhibiting to the public for its delectation and instruction, groups of objects and specimens of cultural value: artistic, historical, scientific and technological collections, botanical and zoological gardens and aquariums.

II. General principles

2. Member States should take all appropriate steps to ensure that the museums on their territory are accessible to all without regard to economic or social status.

3. To that end, account should be taken, in selecting the measures to be applied, of the different forms of museum administration that may exist in individual Member States. The measures might vary, for example, according to whether museums are owned and administered by the State or whether,

even if not State owned, they receive regular or occasional financial assistance from the State, or whether the State participates in their management in a scientific, technical or administrative capacity.

III. Material arrangements in and admission to museums

4. The collections should be made easy for all types of people to appreciate by a clear form of presentation, by the systematic placing of notices or labels giving concise information, by the publication of guide books and folders which provide visitors with such explanations as they require and by the organization of regular guided visits accompanied by a commentary adapted to the various categories of visitors; the guides should be properly qualified persons, preferably appointed through the agency of the bodies referred to in paragraph 16 of this Recommendation; discreet use may be made of apparatus for the reproduction of recorded commentaries.

5. Museums should be open every day and at hours convenient for all categories of visitors, particular account being taken of workers' leisure time. They should be provided with a sufficiently large supervisory staff to permit of a rota system so that the museum can remain open every day without interruption—subject to local conditions and customs—as well as every evening after working hours. They should be installed with the necessary equipment for lighting, heating, etc.

6. Museums should be easily accessible, and should be made as attractive as possible, with a measure of comfort. Provided that the character of the establishment is respected and that visits to the collections are not disturbed thereby, lounges, restaurants, cafés and the like should be provided for the public, preferably within the precincts of the museum (in gardens, on terraces, in suitable basements, etc.) or in the immediate vicinity.

7. Admission should be free whenever possible. In cases where admission is not always free and where it is considered necessary to maintain a small admission fee, even if only a token charge, admission to every museum should be free during at least one day a week, or for an equivalent period.

8. Where an admission fee is charged, it should be waived for persons in low-income groups and for members of large families in those countries in which there exist official methods of identifying these groups.

9. Special facilities should be provided to encourage regular visits, such as reduced subscription fees for a given period entitling the subscriber to an unlimited number of entries to a particular museum or group of museums.

10. Free admission should whenever possible be granted to organized parties —whether of school-children or adults—taking part in educational and cultural programmes, and also to members of the museum or of the associations mentioned in paragraph 17 of this Recommendation.

IV. Publicity for museums

11. Member States should, through the intermediary of either the local authorities or of their own cultural relations or tourist services, and in the context of national education and international relations, do everything in their power to encourage increased visits to museums and to exhibitions arranged therein.

12. (a) Member States should urge national or regional tourist agencies to make it one of their main objectives to encourage increased visits to museums and to devote part of their activities and resources to that end.
    (b) Museums should be invited to make regular use of the services of those agencies and to associate them with their own efforts to extend their social and cultural influence.

V. Place and role of museums in the community

13. Museums should serve as intellectual and cultural centres in their own localities. They should therefore contribute to the intellectual and cultural life of the community, which in turn should be given the opportunity of taking part in the activities and development of the museums. This should apply in particular to museums situated in small towns and villages and whose importance is often out of proportion to their size.

14. Close cultural relations should be established between museums and groups in the community, such as professional organizations, trade unions, and social services in industrial and business enterprises.

15. Co-operation between museums and radio and television services and undertakings should also be established or improved so that museum exhibits can be used for the purposes of adult and school education with the maximum safety precautions.

16. The contribution which museums can make to school and adult education should be recognized and encouraged. It should furthermore be systematized by the establishment of appropriate bodies responsible for establishing official and regular liaison between local educational leaders and museums which,

owing to the nature of their collections, are of particular interest to schools. This co-operation might take the following forms:

(a) Each museum might have on its staff educational specialists, to organize, under the curator's supervision, the use of the museum for educational purposes;

(b) Museums might set up educational departments which would call on the services of teachers;

(c) Joint committees of curators and teachers might be established at local, regional or provincial level to ensure that the best use is made of museums for educational purposes;

(d) Any other measures which would co-ordinate the demands of education and the resources of museums.

17. Member States should promote (in particular by granting legal facilities) the establishment and development of associations of friends of the museum or similar associations able to lend their moral and material support to museums. These associations should be granted such powers and privileges as they require to fulfil their purpose.

18. Member States should encourage the development of museum clubs to encourage young people to take part in various museum activites.

The foregoing is the authentic text of the Recommendation duly adopted by the General Conference of the United Nations Educational, Scientific and Cultural Organization during its eleventh session, which was held in Paris and declared closed the fifteenth day of December 1960.

IN FAITH WHEREOF we have appended our signatures this fifteenth day of December 1960.

The President of the General Conference   *The Director-General*

Recommendation concerning the Safeguarding of the Beauty and Character of Landscapes and Sites[1]

Introduction

This Recommendation is concerned to ensure not only the preservation of the original aspects of natural, rural and urban landscapes and sites, whether natural or man-made, but also as far as is possible, their restoration.

It calls attention both to the scientific and aesthetic importance of landscapes and sites and to the fact that they form a heritage which is a major factor in the living conditions of the general public.

In order to counter the threats of modern life to landscapes and sites, preventive control needs to be established over operations and activities liable to impair them.

The protective measures to be adopted include the incorporation of special provisions in urban and regional development plans, scheduling by zones, scheduling of isolated sites, creation and maintenance of natural reserves and national parks, and acquisition of sites by communities.

Responsibility for preservation measures should be entrusted to specialized services with extensive powers.

The Recommendation further emphasizes the need for vigorous educational action in school and out of school with a view to awakening and developing the public's respect for a heritage which is its own and involving it in the protection of that heritage.

---

1. Adopted on 11 December 1962 by the General Conference of Unesco at its twelfth session, held in Paris.

United Nations Educational, Scientific and
Cultural Organization

Recommendation concerning the Safeguarding of the Beauty and Character of Landscapes and Sites

Adopted by the General Conference at its
twelfth session, Paris, 11 December 1962

The General Conference of the United Nations Educational, Scientific and Cultural Organization, meeting in Paris from 9 November to 12 December 1962, in its twelfth session:

Considering that at all periods men have sometimes subjected the beauty and character of landscapes and sites forming part of their natural environment to damage which has impoverished the cultural, aesthetic and even vital heritage of whole regions in all parts of the world,

Considering that by the cultivation of virgin land, the sometimes ill-regulated development of urban centres, the carrying out of extensive works and vast plans for industrial and commercial development and equipment, modern civilizations have accelerated this trend whose progress was relatively slow up to the last century,

Considering that this phenomenon affects the aesthetic value of landscapes and sites, natural or man-made, and the cultural and scientific importance of wild life,

Considering that, on account of their beauty and character, the safeguarding of landscapes and sites, as defined in this recommendation, is necessary to the life of men for whom they represent a powerful physical, moral and spiritual regenerating influence, while at the same time contributing to the artistic and cultural life of peoples, as innumerable and universally known examples bear witness,

Considering furthermore that landscapes and sites are an important factor in the economic and social life of many countries, and are largely instrumental in ensuring the health of their inhabitants,

Recognizing, however, that due account should be taken of the needs of community life, its evolution and the rapid development of technical progress,

Considering, therefore, that it is highly desirable and urgent to consider and adopt the necessary steps with a view to safeguarding the beauty and character of landscapes and sites everywhere, whenever it is still possible to do so,

Having before it proposals concerning the safeguarding of the beauty and character of landscapes and sites, this question forming item 17.4.2 of the session's agenda,

Having decided at its eleventh session that proposals on this item should be the subject of an international instrument in the form of a recommendation to Member States,

Adopts, on this eleventh day of December 1962, this recommendation.

The General Conference recommends that Member States should apply the following provisions by adopting, in the form of a national law or in some other way, measures designed to give effect in the territories under their jurisdiction to the norms and principles embodied in this recommendation.

The General Conference recommends that Member States should bring this recommendation to the attention of the authorities and bodies concerned with the protection of landscapes and sites and with regional development, and of bodies entrusted with the protection of nature and the development of the tourist trade, together with youth organizations.

The General Conference recommends that Member States should, on dates and in a form to be determined, submit to it reports concerning the implementation of this recommendation.

I. Definition

1. For the purpose of this recommendation, the safeguarding of the beauty and character of landscapes and sites is taken to mean the preservation and, where possible, the restoration of the aspect of natural, rural and urban landscapes and sites, whether natural or man-made, which have a cultural or aesthetic interest or form typical natural surroundings.

2. The provisions of this recommendation are also intended to supplement measures for the protection of nature.

II. General principles

3. The studies and measures to be adopted with a view to the safeguarding of landscapes and sites should extend to the whole territory of a State, and should not be confined to certain selected landscapes or sites.

4. In choosing the measures to be adopted, due account should be taken of the relative significance of the landscapes and sites concerned. These measures might vary in accordance with the character and size of the landscapes and sites, their location and the nature of the dangers with which they are threatened.

5. Protection should not be limited to natural landscapes and sites, but should also extend to landscapes and sites whose formation is due wholly or in part to the work of man. Thus, special provisions should be made to ensure the safeguarding of certain urban landscapes and sites which are, in general, the most threatened, especially by building operations and land speculation. Special protection should be accorded to the approaches to monuments.

6. Measures taken for the safeguarding of landscapes and sites should be both preventive and corrective.

7. Preventive measures should be aimed at protecting sites from dangers which may threaten them. These measures should include, in particular, the supervision of works and activities likely to damage landscapes and sites, for example:
(a) The construction of all types of public and private buildings. These should be designed so as to meet certain aesthetic requirements in respect of the building itself and, while avoiding a facile imitation of certain traditional and picturesque forms, should be in harmony with the general atmosphere which it is desired to safeguard;
(b) The construction of roads;
(c) High or low tension electric lines, power production and transmission plant and equipment, aerodromes, broadcasting and television stations, etc.;
(d) Petrol filling stations;
(e) Advertising hoardings and illuminated signs;
(f) Deforestation, including the destruction of trees contributing to the beauty of the landscape, particularly those lining thoroughfares or avenues;
(g) Pollution of the air and water;
(h) Working of mines and quarries and the disposal of their waste products;
(i) Piping of spring water, irrigation works, dams, channels, aqueducts, river regulation works, etc.;
(j) Camping;
(k) Dumping of worn-out material and waste, and domestic, commercial or industrial scrap.

8. In safeguarding the beauty and character of landscapes and sites, allowance should also be made for the dangers resulting from certain forms of work

and certain activities of present-day life, by reason of the noise which they occasion.

9. Activities likely to mar landscapes or sites in areas that are scheduled or protected in some other way should be sanctioned only if the public or social welfare imperatively requires it.

10. Corrective measures should be aimed at repairing the damage caused to landscapes and sites and, as far as possible, restoring them to their original condition.

11. In order to facilitate the task of the various public services responsible for the safeguarding of landscapes and sites in each State, scientific research institutes shoud be set up to co-operate with the competent authorities with a view to the alignment and codification of the laws and regulations applicable in this matter. These provisions and the results of the work carried out by the research institutes should be published in a single administrative publication brought periodically up to date.

III. Protective measures

12. The safeguarding of landscapes and sites should be ensured by use of the following methods:
(a) General supervision by the responsible authorities;
(b) Insertion of obligations into urban development plans and planning at all levels: regional, rural and urban;
(c) Scheduling of extensive landscapes 'by zones';
(d) Scheduling of isolated sites;
(e) Creation and maintenance of natural reserves and national parks;
(f) Acquisition of sites by communities.

General supervision

13. General supervision should be exercised over works and activities likely to damage landscapes and sites throughout the whole territory of the State.

Town planning and rural planning schemes

14. Urban and rural planning schemes should embody provisions defining the obligations which should be imposed to ensure the safeguarding of landscapes and sites, even unscheduled ones, situated on the territory affected.

15. Urban and rural planning schemes should be drawn up in order of urgency, specifically for towns or regions in process of rapid development, where the protection of the aesthetic or picturesque character of the town or region justifies the establishment of such schemes.

Scheduling of extensive landscapes 'by zones'

16. Extensive landscapes should be scheduled 'by zones'.

17. When, in a scheduled zone, the aesthetic character is of prime importance, scheduling 'by zones' should involve control of plots and observation of certain general requirements of an aesthetic order covering the use of materials, and their colour, height standards, precautions to be taken to conceal disturbances of the soil resulting from the construction of dams and the operation of quarries, and regulations governing the cutting down of trees, etc.

18. Scheduling 'by zones' should be publicized, and general rules to be observed for the safeguarding of scheduled landscapes should be enacted and made public.

19. Scheduling 'by zones' should not, as a rule, involve payment of compensation.

Scheduling of isolated sites

20. Isolated small sites, whether natural or urban, together with portions of a landscape of particular interest, should be scheduled. Areas which provide a fine view, and areas and buildings surrounding an outstanding monument should also be scheduled. Each of these scheduled sites, areas and buildings should be the subject of a special administrative decision of which the owner should be duly notified.

21. Scheduling should mean that the owner is prohibited from destroying the site, or altering its condition or aspect, without permission from the authorities responsible for its protection.

22. When such permission is granted, it should be accompanied by all the conditions necessary to the safeguarding of the site. No permission should be needed, however, for normal agricultural activities, nor for normal maintenance work on buildings.

23. Expropriation by the authorities, together with the carrying out of public works in a scheduled site, should be subject to the agreement of the authorities

responsible for its protection. No-one should be able to acquire, by prescription, within a scheduled site, rights likely to change the character or aspect of the site. No conventionary rights should be granted by the owner without the agreement of the responsible authorities.

24. Scheduling should involve a prohibition on the pollution of the ground, air or water in any way whatsoever, while the extraction of minerals should likewise be subject to special permission.

25. All advertising should be forbidden in a scheduled area and its immediate surroundings, or be limited to special emplacements to be decided by the authorities responsible for the protection of the site.

26. Permission to camp in a scheduled site should, in principle, be refused, or granted only within an area fixed by the responsible authorities and subject to their inspection.

27. Scheduling of a site may entitle the owner to compensation in cases of direct and definite prejudice resulting therefrom.

Natural reserves and national parks

28. When conditions are suitable, Member States should incorporate in the zones and sites to be protected, national parks intended for the education and recreation of the public, or natural reserves, strict or special. Such natural reserves and national parks should form a group of experimental zones intended also for research into the formation and restoration of the landscape and the protection of nature.

Acquisition of sites by communities

29. Member States should encourage the acquisition by communities of areas forming part of a landscape or site which it is desired to protect. When necessary, it should be possible to effect such acquisition by expropriation.

IV. Application of protective measures

30. The fundamental norms and principles governing the protection of landscapes and sites in each Member State should have the force of law, and the measures for their application should be entrusted to the responsible authorities within the framework of the powers conferred on them by law.

31. Member States should set up specialized bodies of an administrative or advisory nature.

32. The administrative bodies should be specialized central or regional departments entrusted with carrying out protective measures. Accordingly, those departments should be in a position to study problems of protection and scheduling, to undertake surveys on the spot, to prepare decisions to be taken and to supervise their implementation. They should likewise be entrusted with proposing measures designed to reduce the dangers which may be involved in carrying out certain types of work or repairing damage caused by such work.

33. The advisory bodies should consist of commissions at national, regional or local level, entrusted with the task of studying questions relating to protection and giving their opinion on those questions to the central or regional authorities or to the local communities concerned. The opinion of these commissions should be sought in all cases and in good time, particularly at the stage of preliminary planning, in the case of large-scale works of public interest, such as the building of highways, the setting up of hydro-technical or new industrial installations, etc.

34. Member States should facilitate the formation and operation of national and local non-governmental bodies, one of whose functions would be to collaborate with the bodies mentioned in paragraphs 31, 32 and 33, particularly by informing the public and warning the appropriate departments of dangers threatening landscapes and sites.

35. Violation of the rules governing the protection of landscapes and sites should involve payment of damages or the obligation to restore the site to its former condition, as far as possible.

36. Administrative or criminal prosecutions should be provided for in the case of deliberate damage to protected landscapes and sites.

V. Education of the public

37. Educational action should be taken in school and out of school with a view to arousing and developing public respect for landscapes and sites and publicizing the regulations laid down to ensure their protection.

38. Teachers to be entrusted with this task in schools should undergo special training in the form of specialized courses in institutions of secondary and higher education.

IV.B.3

39. Member States should also facilitate the work of existing museums, with a view to intensifying the educational action they have already undertaken to this end, and should consider the possibility of establishing special museums, or specialized departments in existing museums, for the study and display of the natural and cultural features of particular regions.

40. The education of the public outside schools should be the task of the press, of private associations for the protection of landscapes and sites or for the protection of nature, of bodies concerned with the tourist trade and of youth or popular education organizations.

41. Member States should facilitate the education of the public and promote the work of associations, bodies and organizations devoted to this task by the supply of material assistance and by making available to them and to educationists in general appropriate publicity media such as films, radio and television programmes, material for permanent, temporary or mobile exhibitions. pamphlets and books suitable for wide distribution and planned on educational lines. Wide publicity could be provided through journals and magazines and regional periodicals.

42. National and international 'days', competitions and similar occasions should be devoted to encouraging the appreciation of natural or man-made landscapes and sites in order to direct public attention to the fact that the protection of their beauty and character is of prime importance to the community.

The foregoing is the authentic text of the Recommendation duly adopted by the General Conference of the United Nations Educational, Scientific and Cultural Organization during its twelfth session, which was held in Paris and declared closed the twelfth day of December 1962.

IN FAITH WHEREOF we have appended our signatures this eighteenth day of December 1962.

The President of the General Conference　　　　　　*The Director-General*

Recommendation on the Means of Prohibiting and Preventing the Illicit Export, Import and Transfer of Ownership of Cultural Property [1]

Introduction

The desire to acquire works of art and the considerable profits which can be made on some acquisitions, coupled with the scientific and artistic interest which they arouse, have long induced many dealers and private or even public collectors, as well as some museums, to overlook the illicit conditions in which the objects have been acquired and exported from their country of origin. The purpose of the Recommendation is to protect the national cultural heritage of States by countering the illicit operations which threaten it.

The Recommendation stipulates that each Member State should define which items of cultural property within its territory should receive the protection provided for by the Recommendation. Steps should be taken to exert effective control over the export and import of cultural property. In particular, no import of cultural property should be authorized until such property has been cleared from any restrictions on the part of the exporting State.

With regard to a field in which close co-operation between governments is a necessity, the Recommendation provides that States should conclude among themselves bilateral or multilateral agreements to overcome the many problems encountered, particularly those arising from the illicit export of items of cultural property from the national territory and the return of such property to the country of origin. In 1970, the General Conference of Unesco accordingly adopted an international convention for that purpose.

---

1. Adopted on 19 November 1964 by the General Conference of Unesco at its thirteenth session, held in Paris.

United Nations Educational, Scientific and
Cultural Organization

Recommendation on the Means of Prohibiting and Preventing the Illicit Export, Import and Transfer of Ownership of Cultural Property

Adopted by the General Conference at its
thirteenth session, Paris, 19 November 1964

The General Conference of the United Nations Educational, Scientific and Cultural Organization, meeting in Paris from 20 October to 20 November 1964, at its thirteenth session,

Being of the opinion that cultural property constitutes a basic element of civilization and national culture, and that familiarity with it leads to understanding and mutual appreciation between nations,

Considering that it is incumbent upon every State to protect the cultural property existing within its territory and which constitutes its national heritage against the dangers resulting from illicit export, import and transfer of ownership,

Considering that, to avert these dangers, it is essential for every Member State to become increasingly alive to the moral obligations to respect its own cultural heritage and that of all nations,

Considering that the objectives in view cannot be achieved without close collaboration among Member States,

Convinced that steps should be taken to encourage the adoption of appropriate measures and to improve the climate of international solidarity without which the objectives in view would not be attained,

Having before it proposals for international regulations to prohibit and prevent the illicit export, import and transfer of ownership of cultural property, which constitutes item 15.3.3 on the agenda of the session,

Having decided, at its twelfth session, that these proposals should be regulated at the international level by way of a recommendation to Member States, while expressing the hope that an international convention may be adopted as soon as possible,

Adopts, this nineteenth day of November 1964, this recommendation.

The General Conference recommends that Member States should apply the following provisions by taking whatever legislative or other steps may be required to give effect, within their respective territories, to the principles and norms formulated in this recommendation.

The General Conference recommends that Member States should bring this recommendation to the knowledge of authorities and organizations concerned with the protection of cultural property.

The General Conference recommends that Member States should report to it, on dates and in a manner to be determined by it, on the action which they have taken to give effect to this recommendation.

I. Definition

1. For the purpose of this recommendation, the term 'cultural property' means movable and immovable property of great importance to the cultural heritage of a country, such as works of art and architecture, manuscripts, books and other property of artistic, historical or archaeological interest, ethnological documents, type specimens of flora and fauna, scientific collections and important collections of books and archives, including musical archives.

2. Each Member State should adopt whatever criteria it deems most suitable for defining which items of cultural property within its territory should receive the protection envisaged in this recommendation by reason of their great importance.

II. General principles

3. To ensure the protection of its cultural heritage against all dangers of impoverishment, each Member State should take appropriate steps to exert effective control over the export of cultural property as defined in paragraphs 1 and 2.

4. No import of cultural property should be authorized until such property has been cleared from any restrictions on the part of the competent authorities in the exporting State.

5. Each Member State should take appropriate steps to prevent the illicit transfer of ownership of cultural property.

6. Each Member State should lay down rules governing the application of the above principles.

7. Any export, import or transfer of ownership effected contrary to the rules adopted by each Member State in accordance with paragraph 6 should be regarded as illicit.

8. Museums, and in general all services and institutions concerned with the conservation of cultural property, should refrain from purchasing any item of cultural property obtained through an illicit export, import or transfer of ownership.

9. In order to encourage and facilitate legitimate exchange of cultural property, Member States should strive to make available to public collections in other Member States, by sale or exchange, objects of the same type as those the export or transfer of ownership of which cannot be authorized, or certain of the latter objects, on loan or deposit.

III. Measures recommended

Recognition and national inventory of cultural property

10. To ensure more effective application of the above general principles, each Member State should, as far as possible, devise and apply procedures for the recognition of the cultural property, as defined in paragraphs 1 and 2 above, which exists within its territory, and draw up a national inventory of such property. The inclusion of a cultural object in this inventory should produce no change in the legal ownership of that object. In particular, a cultural object in private ownership should remain such even after inclusion in the national inventory. This inventory would not be of a restrictive character.

Institutions for the protection of cultural property

11. Each Member State should provide that the protection of cultural property shall be the concern of appropriate official bodies and, if necessary, should set up a national service for the protection of cultural property. Although differences of constitutional provisions and tradition and disparity of resources preclude the adoption by all Member States of a uniform structure, certain common principles, set forth below, should nevertheless be adopted if the creation of a national service for the protection of cultural property be considered necessary:
(a) The national service for the protection of cultural property should, as far as possible, take the form of a State-operated administrative service, or a body operating in accordance with the national law with the necessary administrative, technical and financial means to exercise its functions effectively.

(b) The functions of the national service for the protection of cultural property should include:

   (i) Recognition of the cultural property existing within the territory of the State, and, where appropriate, the establishment and maintenance of a national inventory of such property, in accordance with the provisions of paragraph 10 above;

   (ii) Co-operation with other competent bodies in the control of the export, import and transfer of ownership of cultural property, in accordance with the provisions of Section II above; the control of exports would be considerably facilitated if items of cultural property were accompanied, at the time of export, by an appropriate certificate in which the exporting State would certify that the export of the cultural property is authorized. In case of doubt regarding the legality of the export, the institution entrusted with the protection of cultural property should address itself to the competent institution with a view to confirming the legality of the export.

(c) The national service for the protection of cultural property should be empowered to submit proposals to the competent national authorities for any other appropriate legislative or administrative measures for the protection of cultural property, including sanctions for the prevention of illicit export, import and transfer of ownership.

(d) The national service for the protection of cultural property should be able to call upon experts to advise it on technical problems and to propose solutions in contentious cases.

12. Each Member State should, in so far as necessary, set up a fund or take other appropriate financial measures in order to have means necessary to purchase exceptionally important cultural property.

Bilateral and multilateral agreements

13. Whenever necessary or desirable, Member States should conclude bilateral or multilateral agreements, within the framework of regional intergovernmental organizations for instance, to resolve problems flowing from the export, import or transfer of ownership of cultural property, and more especially in order to secure the restitution of cultural property illicitly exported from the territory of a party to the agreements and located in the territory of another. Such agreements might, where appropriate, be comprised within agreements of wider scope, such as cultural agreements.

International collaboration in the detection of illicit operations

14. Whenever necessary or desirable, these bilateral or multilateral agreements should include provisions to the effect that whenever it is proposed to transfer the ownership of a cultural object the competent services of each State shall ascertain that there are no grounds for regarding that object as proceeding from a theft, an illicit export or transfer of ownership, or any other operation regarded as illegal under the legislation of the exporting State, for instance, by requiring the presentation of the certificate referred to in paragraph 11. Any dubious offer, and any details relating thereto, should be brought to the knowledge of the services concerned.

15. Member States should endeavour to assist each other by exchanging the fruits of their experience in the fields covered by this recommendation.

Restitution or return of illicitly exported cultural property

16. Member States, services for the protection of cultural property, museums and, in general, all competent institutions should collaborate with one another in ensuring or facilitating the restitution or return of cultural objects illicitly exported. This restitution or return should be carried out in accordance with the laws in force in the State on whose territory the objects are located.

Publicity in the event of the disappearance of a cultural object

17. The disappearance of any cultural object should, at the request of the State claiming that object, be brought to the knowledge of the public by means of appropriate publicity.

Rights of bona fide *purchasers*

18. Each Member State should, if necessary, take appropriate measures to provide that its internal laws or the international conventions to which it may become a party, ensure to the *bona fide* purchaser of cultural property which is to be restored or returned to the territory of the State from which it had been illegally exported, the possibility of obtaining damages or fair compensation.

Educational action

19. In a spirit of international collaboration which would take into account both the universal nature of culture and the necessity of exchanges for enab-

ling all to benefit by the cultural heritage of mankind, each Member State should take steps to stimulate and develop among its nationals interest in and respect for the cultural heritage of all nations. Such action should be undertaken by the competent services in co-operation with the educational services and with the Press and other media for the communication and dissemination of information, youth and adult education organizations and groups and individuals concerned with cultural activities.

The foregoing is the authentic text of the Recommendation duly adopted by the General Conference of the United Nations Educational, Scientific and Cultural Organization during its thirteenth session, which was held in Paris and declared closed the twentieth day of November 1964.

IN FAITH WHEREOF we have appended our signatures this twenty-first day of November 1964.

The President of the General Conference   *The Director-General*

Recommendation concerning the Preservation of Cultural Property Endangered by Public or Private Works[1]

Introduction

This Recommendation was adopted as a result of the deep concern aroused the world over by the danger that the operations at the High Dam on the Nile would cause the submersion and destruction of the magnificent temples built upstream from Aswan, more than three thousand years ago, as well as of the neighbouring archaeological sites.

This Recommendation recognizes that it is essential to harmonize the preservation of the cultural heritage with the changes necessitated by social and economic development. To meet this twofold requirement, it advocates the establishment of an inventory of important items of cultural property, priority being given to property situated in areas where it is endangered by public or private works. This identification of important cultural property should make it possible to assess in advance the repercussions of any decisions to initiate major works in places where the heritage to be safeguarded is situated and to take the necessary steps to protect it. The Recommendation urges the preservation of property in situ, *that is, in the place in which it is situated. It states, however, that when overriding economical or social conditions require that cultural property be transferred, abandoned or destroyed, a careful study should be made and records prepared and made available for future research.*

The cost of preservation should be met from special budgets or from part of the budget of major public or private works to be carried out.

---

1. Adopted on 19 November 1968 by the General Conference of Unesco at its fifteenth session, held in Paris.

United Nations Educational, Scientific and
Cultural Organization

Recommendation concerning the Preservation of Cultural Property Endangered by Public or Private Works

Adopted by the General Conference at its
fifteenth session, Paris, 19 November 1968

The General Conference of the United Nations Educational, Scientific and Cultural Organization, meeting in Paris from 15 October to 20 November 1968, at its fifteenth session,

Considering that contemporary civilization and its future evolution rest upon, among other elements, the cultural traditions of the peoples of the world, their creative force and their social and economic development,

Considering that cultural property is the product and witness of the different traditions and of the spiritual achievements of the past and thus is an essential element in the personality of the peoples of the world,

Considering that it is indispensable to preserve it as much as possible, according to its historical and artistic importance, so that the significance and message of cultural property become a part of the spirit of peoples who thereby may gain consciousness of their own dignity,

Considering that preserving cultural property and rendering it accessible constitute, in the spirit of the Declaration of the Principles of International Cultural Co-operation adopted on 4 November 1966 in the course of its fourteenth session, means of encouraging mutual understanding among peoples and thereby serve the cause of peace,

Considering also that the well-being of all peoples depends, *inter alia*, upon the existence of a favourable and stimulating environment and that the preservation of cultural property of all periods of history contributes directly to such an environment,

Recognizing, on the other hand, the rôle that industrialization, towards which world civilization is moving, plays in the development of peoples and their spiritual and national fulfilment,

Considering, however, that the prehistoric, protohistoric and historic monuments and remains, as well as numerous recent structures having artistic, historic or scientific importance are increasingly threatened by public and private works resulting from industrial development and urbanization,

Considering that it is the duty of governments to ensure the protection and the preservation of the cultural heritage of mankind, as much as to promote social and economic development,

Considering in consequence that it is urgent to harmonize the preservation of the cultural heritage with the changes which follow from social and economic development, making serious efforts to meet both requirements in a broad spirit of understanding, and with reference to appropriate planning,

Considering equally that adequate preservation and accessibility of cultural property constitute a major contribution to the social and economic development of countries and regions which possess such treasures of mankind by means of promoting national and international tourism,

Considering finally that the surest guarantee for the preservation of cultural property rests in the respect and the attachment felt for it by the people themselves, and persuaded that such feelings may be greatly strengthened by adequate measures carried out by Member States,

Having before it proposals concerning the preservation of cultural property endangered by public or private works, which constitute item 16 on the agenda of the session,

Having decided at its thirteenth session that proposals on this item should be the subject of an international instrument in the form of a recommendation to Member States,

Adopts on this nineteenth day of November 1968 this recommendation.

The General Conference recommends that Member States should apply the following provisions by taking whatever legislative or other steps may be required to give effect within their respective territories to the norms and principles set forth in this recommendation.

The General Conference recommends that Member States should bring this recommendation to the attention of the authorities or services responsible for public or private works as well as to the bodies responsible for the conservation and the protection of monuments and historic, artistic, archaeological and scientific sites. It recommends that authorities and bodies which plan programmes for education and the development of tourism be equally informed.

The General Conference recommends that Member States should report to it, on the dates and in a manner to be determined by it, on the action they have taken to give effect to this recommendation.

I. Definition

1.   For the purpose of this recommendation, the term 'cultural property' applies to:
(a)   Immovables, such as archaeological and historic or scientific sites, structures or other features of historic, scientific, artistic or architectural value, whether religious or secular, including groups of traditional structures, historic quarters in urban or rural built-up areas and the ethnological structures of previous cultures still extant in valid form. It applies to such immovables constituting ruins existing above the earth as well as to archaeological or historic remains found within the earth. The term cultural property also includes the setting of such property;
(b)   Movable property of cultural importance including that existing in or recovered from immovable property and that concealed in the earth, which may be found in archaeological or historical sites or elsewhere.

2.   The term 'cultural property' includes not only the established and scheduled architectural, archaelogical and historic sites and structure, but also the unscheduled or unclassified vestiges of the past as well as artistically or historically important recent sites and structures.

II. General principles

3.   Measures to preserve cultural property should extend to the whole territory of the State and should not be confined to certain monuments and sites.

4.   Protective inventories of important cultural property, whether scheduled or unscheduled, should be maintained. Where such inventories do not exist, priority should be given in their establishment to the thorough survey of cultural property in areas where such property is endangered by public or private works.

5.   Due account should be taken of the relative significance of the cultural property concerned when determining measures required for the:
(a)   Preservation of an entire site, structure, or other forms of immovable cultural property from the effects of private or public works;
(b)   Salvage or rescue of cultural property if the area in which it is found is to be transformed by public or private works, and the whole or a part of the property in question is to be preserved and removed.

6.   Measures should vary according to the character, size and location of the cultural property and the nature of the dangers with which it is threatened.

IV.B.5

7. Measures for the preservation or salvage of cultural property should be preventive and corrective.

8. Preventive and corrective measures should be aimed at protecting or saving cultural property from public or private works likely to damage and destroy it, such as:

(a) Urban expansion and renewal projects, although they may retain scheduled monuments while sometimes removing less important structures, with the result that historical relations and the setting of historic quarters are destroyed;

(b) Similar projects in areas where groups of traditional structures having cultural value as a whole risk being destroyed for the lack of a scheduled individual monument;

(c) Injudicious modifications and repair of individual historic buildings;

(d) The construction or alteration of highways which are a particular danger to sites or to historically important structures or groups of structures;

(e) The construction of dams for irrigation, hydroelectric power or flood control;

(f) The construction of pipelines and of power and transmission lines of electricity;

(g) Farming operations including deep ploughing, drainage and irrigation operations, the clearing and levelling of land and afforestation;

(h) Works required by the growth of industry and the technological progress of industrialized societies such as airfields, mining and quarrying operations and dredging and reclamation of channels and harbours.

9. Member States should give due priority to measures required for the preservation *in situ* of cultural property endangered by public or private works in order to preserve historical associations and continuity. When overriding economic or social conditions require that cultural property be transferred, abandoned or destroyed, the salvage or rescue operations should always include careful study of the cultural property involved and the preparations of detailed records.

10. The results of studies having scientific or historic value carried out in connexion with salvage operations, particularly when all or much of the immovable cultural property has been abandoned or destroyed, should be published or otherwise made available for future research.

11. Important structures and other monuments which have been transferred in order to save them from destruction by public or private works should be placed on a site or in a setting which resembles their former position and natural, historic or artistic associations.

12. Important movable cultural property, including representative samples of objects recovered from archaeological excavations, obtained from salvage operations should be preserved for study or placed on exhibition in institutions such as museums, including site museums, or universities.

III. Preservation and salvage measures

13. The preservation or salvage of cultural property endangered by public or private works should be ensured through the means mentioned below, the precise measures to be determined by the legislation and organizational system of the State:
(a) Legislation;
(b) Finance;
(c) Administrative measures;
(d) Procedures to preserve and to salvage cultural property;
(e) Penalties;
(f) Repairs;
(g) Awards;
(h) Advice;
(i) Educational programmes.

Legislation

14. Member States should enact or maintain on the national as well as on the local level the legislative measures necessary to ensure the preservation or salvage of cultural property endangered by public or private works in accordance with the norms and principles embodied in this recommendation.

Finance

15. Member States should ensure that adequate budgets are available for the preservation or salvage of cultural property endangered by public or private works. Although differences in legal systems and traditions as well as disparity in resources preclude the adoption of uniform measures, the following should be considered:
(a) The national or local authorities responsible for the safeguarding of cultural property should have adequate budgets to undertake the preservation or salvage of cultural property endangered by public or private works; or
(b) The costs of preserving or salvaging cultural property endangered by public or private works, including preliminary archaeological research, should form part of the budget of construction costs; or

(c) The possibility of combining the two methods mentioned in sub-paragraphs a and b above should be provided for.

16. In the event of unusual costs due to the size and complexity of the operations required, there should be possibilities of obtaining additional funds through enabling legislation, special subventions, a national fund for monuments or other appropriate means. The services responsible for the safeguarding of cultural property should be empowered to administer or to utilize these extra-budgetary contributions required for the preservation or salvage of cultural property endangered by public or private works.

17. Member States should encourage proprietors of artistically or historically important structures, including structures forming part of a traditional group, or residents in a historic quarter in urban or rural built-up areas to preserve the character and aesthetic qualities of their cultural property, which would otherwise be endangered by public or private works, through:
(a) Favourable tax rates; or
(b) The establishment, through appropriate legislation, of a budget to assist, by grants, loans or other measures, local authorities, institutions and private owners of artistically, architecturally, scientifically or historically important structures including groups of traditional structures to maintain or to adapt them suitably for functions which would meet the needs of contemporary society; or
(c) The possibility of combining the two methods mentioned in sub-paragraphs a and b above should be provided for.

18. If the cultural property is not scheduled or otherwise protected it should be possible for the owner to request such assistance from the appropriate authorities.

19. National or local authorities, as well as private owners, when budgeting for the preservation of cultural property endangered by public or private works, should take into account the intrinsic value of cultural property and also the contribution it can make to the economy as a tourist attraction.

Administrative measures

20. Responsibility for the preservation or salvage of cultural property endangered by public or private works should be entrusted to appropriate official bodies. Whenever official bodies or services already exist for the protection of cultural property, these bodies or services should be given responsibility for the preservation of cultural property against the dangers caused by public or

private works. If such services do not exist, special bodies or services should be created for the purpose of the preservation of cultural property endangered by public or private works; and although differences of constitutional provisions and traditions preclude the adoption of a uniform system, certain common principles should be adopted.

(a) There should be a co-ordinating or consultative body, composed of representatives of the authorities responsible for the safeguarding of cultural property, for public and private works, for town planning, and of research and educational institutions, which should be competent to advise of the preservation of cultural property endangered by public or private works and, in particular, on conflicts of interest between requirements for public or private works and the preservation or salvage of cultural property.

(b) Provincial, municipal or other forms of local government should also have services responsible for the preservation or salvage of cultural property endangered by public or private works. These services should be able to call upon the assistance of national services or other appropriate bodies in accordance with their capabilities and requirements.

(c) The services responsible for the safeguarding of cultural property should be adequately staffed with the specialists required for the preservation or salvage of cultural property endangered by public or private works, such as architects, urbanists, archaeologists, historians, inspectors and other specialists and technicians.

(d) Administrative measures should be taken to co-ordinate the work of the different services responsible for the safeguarding of cultural property with that of other services responsible for public and private works and that of any other department or service whose responsibilites touch upon the problem of the preservation or salvage of cultural property endangered by public or private works.

(e) Administrative measures should be taken to establish an authority or commission in charge of urban development programmes in all communities having scheduled or unscheduled historic quarters, sites and monuments which need to be preserved against public and private construction.

21. At the preliminary survey stage of any project involving construction in a locality recognized as being of cultural interest or likely to contain objects of archaeological or historical importance, several variants of the project should be prepared, at regional or municipal level, before a decision is taken. The choice between these variants should be made on the basis of a comprehensive comparative analysis, in order that the most advantageous solution, both economically and from the point of view of preserving or salvaging cultural property, may be adopted.

Procedures to preserve and to salvage cultural property

22. Thorough surveys should be carried out well in advance of any public or private works which might endanger cultural property to determine:

(a) The measures to be taken to preserve important cultural property *in situ;*

(b) The amount of salvage operations which would be required such as the selection of archaeological sites to be excavated, structures to be transferred and movable cultural property salvaged, etc.

23. Measures for the preservation or salvage of cultural property should be carried out well in advance of public or private works. In areas of archaeological or cultural importance, such as historic towns, villages, sites and districts, which should be protected by the legislation of every country, the starting of new work should be made conditional upon the execution of preliminary archaeological excavations. If necessary, work should be delayed to ensure that adequate measures are taken for the preservation or salvage of the cultural property concerned.

24. Important archaeological sites, and, in particular, prehistoric sites as they are difficult to recognize, historic quarters in urban or rural areas, groups of traditional structures, ethnological structures of previous cultures and other immovable cultural property which would otherwise be endangered by public or private works should be protected by zoning or scheduling:

(a) Archaeological reserves should be zoned or scheduled and, if necessary, immovable property purchased, to permit thorough excavation or the preservation of the ruins found at the site.

(b) Historic quarters in urban or rural centres and groups of traditional structures should be zoned and appropriate regulations adopted to preserve their setting and character, such as the imposition of controls on the degree to which historically or artistically important structures can be renovated and the type and design of new structures which can be introduced. The preservation of monuments should be an absolute requirement of any well-designed plan for urban redevelopment especially in historic cities or districts. Similar regulations should cover the area surrounding a scheduled monument or site and its setting to preserve its association and character. Due allowance should be made for the modification of ordinary regulations applicable to new construction; these should be placed in abeyance when new structures are introduced into an historical zone. Ordinary types of commercial advertising by means of posters and illuminated announcements should be forbidden, but commercial establishments could be allowed to indicate their presence by means of judiciously presented signs.

25. Member States should make it obligatory for persons finding archaeological remains in the course of public or private works to declare them at the earliest possible moment to the competent service. Careful examination should be carried out by the service concerned and, if the site is important, construction should be deferred to permit thorough excavation, due allowance or compensation being made for the delays incurred.

26. Member States should have provisions for the acquisition, through purchase, by national or local governments and other appropriate bodies of important cultural property endangered by public or private works. When necessary, it should be possible to effect such acquisition through expropriation.

Penalties

27. Member States should take steps to ensure that offences, through intent or negligence, against the preservation or salvage of cultural property endangered by public or private works are severely punished by their Penal Code, which should provide for fines or imprisonment or both.

In addition, the following measures could be applied:
(a) Whenever possible, restoration of the site or structure at the expense of those responsible for the damage to it;
(b) In the case of a chance archaeological find, payment of damages to the State when immovable cultural property has been damaged, destroyed or neglected; confiscation without compensation when a movable object has been concealed.

Repairs

28. Member States should, when the nature of the property so allows, adopt the necessary measures to ensure the repair, restoration or reconstruction of cultural property damaged by public or private works. They should also foresee the possibility of requiring local authorities and private owners of important cultural property to carry out repairs or restorations, with technical and financial assistance if necessary.

Awards

29. Member States should encourage individuals, associations and municipalities to take part in programmes for the preservation or salvage of cultural property endangered by public or private works. Measures to that effect could include:

(a) *Ex gratia* payments to individuals reporting or surrendering hidden archaeological finds;

(b) Awards of certificates, medals or other forms of recognition to individuals, even if they belong to government service, associations, institutions or municipalities which have carried out outstanding projects for the preservation or salvage of cultural property endangered by public or private works.

Advice

30. Member States should provide individuals, associations or municipalities lacking the required experience or staff with technical advice or supervision to maintain adequate standards for the preservation or salvage of cultural property endangered by public or private works.

Educational programmes

31. In a spirit of international collaboration, Member States should take steps to stimulate and develop among their nationals interest in, and respect for, the cultural heritage of the past of their own and other traditions in order to preserve or to salvage cultural property endangered by public or private works.

32. Specialized publications, articles in the press and radio and television broadcasts should publicize the nature of the dangers to cultural property arising from ill-conceived public or private works as well as cases where cultural property has been successfully preserved or salvaged.

33. Educational institutions, historical and cultural associations, public bodies concerned with the tourist industry and associations for popular education should have programmes to publicize the dangers to cultural property arising from short-sighted public or private works, and to underline the fact that projects to preserve cultural property contribute to international understanding.

34. Museums and educational institutions and other interested organizations should prepare special exhibitions on the dangers to cultural property arising from uncontrolled public or private works and on the measures which have been used to preserve or to salvage cultural property which has been endangered.

The foregoing is the authentic text of the recommendation duly adopted by the General Conference of the United Nations Educational, Scientific and

Cultural Organization during its fifteenth session, which was held in Paris and declared closed the twentieth day of November 1968.

IN FAITH WHEREOF we have appended our signatures this twenty-second day of November 1968.

The President of General Conference   *The Director-General*

IV.B.5

Recommendation concerning the Protection, at National Level, of the Cultural and Natural Heritage[1]

Introduction

Unlike the Convention on the world heritage, the aim of which is to preserve sites of universal importance, the Recommendation is intended to induce States to safeguard all the components of their cultural and natural heritage.

The protection that should be enjoyed by such property under the Recommendation includes its identification, study, conservation, restoration, effective presentation, and integration into contemporary society.

It is essential to list the various items of property that make up the cultural and natural heritage. The Recommendation provides for the keeping of an up-to-date inventory and the preparation of maps and of appropriate documentation. It affirms that States should draw up carefully planned programmes for the conservation and presentation of their cultural heritage with a view to preserving its traditional appearance. Likewise, with regard to the natural heritage, programmes should be prepared for the restoration of scheduled areas that have been damaged by industry or other human activities.

Protection of the cultural and natural heritage should be entrusted to specialized services assisted by advisory bodies.

---

1. Adopted on 16 November 1972 by the General Conference of Unesco at its seventeenth session, held in Paris.

United Nations Educational, Scientific and
Cultural Organization

Recommendation concerning the Protection, at National Level, of the Cultural and Natural Heritage

Adopted by the General Conference at its seventeenth session, Paris, 16 November 1972

The General Conference of the United Nations Educational, Scientific and Cultural Organization, meeting in Paris, at its seventeenth session, from 17 October to 21 November 1972,

Considering that, in a society where living conditions are changing at an accelerated pace, it is essential for man's equilibrium and development to preserve for him a fitting setting in which to live, where he will remain in contact with nature and the evidences of civilization bequeathed by past generations, and that, to this end, it is appropriate to give the cultural and natural heritage an active function in community life and to integrate into an overall policy the achievements of our time, the values of the past and the beauty of nature,

Considering that such integration into social and economic life must be one of the fundamental aspects of regional development and national planning at every level,

Considering that particularly serious dangers engendered by new phenomena peculiar to our times are threatening the cultural and natural heritage, which constitute an essential feature of mankind's heritage and a source of enrichment and harmonious development for present and future civilization,

Considering that each item of the cultural and natural heritage is unique and that the disappearance of any one item constitutes a definite loss and an irreversible impoverishment of that heritage.

Considering that every country in whose territory there are components of the cultural and natural heritage has an obligation to safeguard this part of mankind's heritage and to ensure that it is handed down to future generations,

Considering that the study, knowledge and protection of the cultural and natural heritage in the various countries of the world are conducive to mutual understanding among the peoples,

Considering that the cultural and natural heritage forms an harmonious whole, the components of which are indissociable,

Considering that a policy for the protection of the cultural and natural heritage, thought out and formulated in common, is likely to bring about a continuing interaction among Member States and to have a decisive effect on the activities of the United Nations Educational, Scientific and Cultural Organization in this field,

Noting that the General Conference has already adopted international instruments for the protection of the cultural and natural heritage, such as the Recommendation on International Principles Applicable to Archaeological Excavations (1956), the Recommendation concerning the Safeguarding of the Beauty and Character of Landscapes and Sites (1962) and the Recommendation concerning the Preservation of Cultural Property Endangered by Public or Private Works (1968),

Desiring to supplement and extend the application of the standards and principles laid down in such recommendations,

Having before it proposals concerning the protection of the cultural and natural heritage, which question appears on the agenda of the session as item 23,

Having decided, at its sixteenth session, that this question should be made the subject of international regulations, to take the form of a recommendation to Member States,

Adopts this sixteenth day of November 1972, this Recommendation.

I. Definitions of the cultural and the natural heritage

1. For the purposes of this Recommendation, the following shall be considered as 'cultural heritage':

monuments: architectural works, works of monumental sculpture and painting, including cave dwellings and inscriptions, and elements, groups of elements or structures of special value from the point of view of archaeology, history, art or science;

groups of buildings: groups of separate or connected buildings which, because of their architecture, their homogeneity or their place in the landscape, are of special value from the point of view of history, art or science;

sites: topographical areas, the combined works of man and of nature, which are of special value by reason of their beauty or their interest from the archaeological, historical, ethnological or anthropological points of view.

2. For the purposes of this Recommendation, the following shall be considered as 'natural heritage':

natural features consisting of physical and biological formations or groups of such formations, which are of special value from the aesthetic or scientific point of view;

geological and physiographical formations and precisely delineated areas which constitute the habitat of species of animals and plants, valuable or threatened, of special value from the point of view of science or conservation;

natural sites or precisely delineated natural areas of special value from the point of view of science, conservation or natural beauty, or in their relation to the combined works of man and of nature.

II. National policy

3. In conformity with their jurisdictional and legislative requirements, each State should formulate, develop and apply as far as possible a policy whose principal aim should be to co-ordinate and make use of all scientific, technical, cultural and other resources available to secure the effective protection, conservation and presentation of the cultural and natural heritage.

III. General principles

4. The cultural and natural heritage represents wealth, the protection, conservation and presentation of which impose responsibilities on the States in whose territory it is situated, both vis-à-vis their own nationals and vis-à-vis the international community as a whole; Member States should take such action as may be necessary to meet these responsibilites.

5. The cultural or natural heritage should be considered in its entirety as a homogeneous whole, comprising not only works of great intrinsic value, but also more modest items that have, with the passage of time, acquired cultural or natural value.

6. None of these works and none of these items should, as a general rule, be dissociated from its environment.

7. As the ultimate purpose of protecting, conserving and presenting the cultural and natural heritage is the development of man, Member States should, as far as possible, direct their work in this field in such a way that the cultural and natural heritage may no longer be regarded as a check on national development but as a determining factor in such development.

IV.B.6

8. The protection, conservation and effective presentation of the cultural and natural heritage should be considered as one of the essential aspects of regional development plans, and planning in general, at the national, regional or local level.

9. An active policy for the conservation of the cultural and natural heritage and for giving it a place in community life should be developed. Member States should arrange for concerted action by all the public and private services concerned, with a view to drawing up and applying such a policy. Preventive and corrective measures relating to the cultural and natural heritage should be supplemented by others, designed to give each of the components of this heritage a function which will make it a part of the nation's social, economic, scientific and cultural life for the present and future, compatible with the cultural or natural character of the item in question. Action for the protection of the cultural and natural heritage should take advantage of scientific and technical advances in all branches of study involved in the protection, conservation and presentation of the cultural or natural heritage.

10. Increasingly significant financial resources should, as far as possible, be made available by the public authorities for the safeguarding and presentation of the cultural and natural heritage.

11. The general public of the area should be associated with the measures to be taken for protection and conservation and should be called on for suggestions and help, with particular reference to regard for and surveillance of the cultural and natural heritage. Consideration might also be given to the possibility of financial support from the private sector.

IV. Organization of services

12. Although their diversity makes it impossible for all Member States to adopt a standard form of organization, certain common criteria should nevertheless be observed.

Specialized public services

13. With due regard for the conditions appropriate to each country, Member States should set up in their territory, wherever they do not already exist, one or more specialized public services to be responsible for the efficient discharge of the following functions:
(a) developing and putting into effect measures of all kinds designed for the protection, conservation and presentation of the country's cultural and natural heritage and for making it an active factor in the life of the com-

munity; and primarily, compiling an inventory of the cultuɪ٫l and natural heritage and establishing appropriate documentation services;
(b) training and recruiting scientific, technical and administrative staff as required, to be responsible for working out identification, protection, conservation and integration programmes and directing their execution;
(c) organizing close co-operation among specialists of various disciplines to study the technical conservation problems of the cultural and natural heritage;
(d) using or creating laboratories for the study of all the scientific problems arising in connexion with the conservation of the cultural and natural heritage;
(e) ensuring that owners or tenants carry out the necessary restoration work and provide for the upkeep of the buildings in the best artistic and technical conditions.

Advisory bodies

14. The specialized services should work with bodies of experts responsible for giving advice on the preparation of measures relating to the cultural and natural heritage. Such bodies should include experts, representatives of the major preservation societies, and representatives of the administrations concerned.

Co-operation among the various bodies

15. The specialized services dealing with the protection, conservation and presentation of the cultural and natural heritage should carry out their work in liaison and on an equal footing with other public services, more particularly those responsible for regional development planning, major public works, the environment, and economic and social planning. Tourist development programmes involving the cultural and natural heritage should be carefully drawn up so as not to impair the intrinsic character and importance of that heritage, and steps should be taken to establish appropriate liaison between the authorities concerned.

16. Continuing co-operation at all levels should be organized among the specialized services whenever large-scale projects are involved, and appropriate co-ordinating arrangements made so that decisions may be taken in concert, taking account of the various interests involved. Provision should be made for joint planning from the start of the studies and machinery developed for the settlement of conflicts.

IV.B.6

Competence of central, federal, regional and local bodies

17. Considering the fact that the problems involved in the protection, conservation and presentation of the cultural and natural heritage are difficult to deal with, calling for special knowledge and sometimes entailing hard choices, and that there are not enough specialized staff available in this field, responsibilities in all matters concerning the devising and execution of protective measures in general should be divided among central or federal and regional or local authorities on the basis of a judicious balance adapted to the situation that exists in each State.

V. Protective measures

18. Member States should, as far as possible, take all necessary scientific, technical and administrative, legal and financial measures to ensure the protection of the cultural and natural heritage in their territories. Such measures should be determined in accordance with the legislation and organization of the State.

Scientific and technical measures

19. Member States should arrange for careful and constant maintenance of their cultural and natural heritage in order to avoid having to undertake the costly operations necessitated by its deterioration; for this purpose, they should provide for regular surveillance of the components of their heritage by means of periodic inspections. They should also draw up carefully planned programmes of conservation and presentation work, gradually taking in all the cultural and natural heritage, depending upon the scientific, technical and financial means at their disposal.

20. Any work required should be preceded and accompanied by such thorough studies as its importance may necessitate. Such studies should be carried out in co-operation with or by specialists in all related fields.

21. Member States should investigate effective methods of affording added protection to those components of the cultural and natural heritage that are threatened by unusually serious dangers. Such methods should take account of the interrelated scientific, technical and artistic problems involved and make it possible to determine the treatment to be applied.

22. These components of the cultural and natural heritage should, in addition, be restored, wherever appropriate, to their former use or given a new and more suitable function, provided that their cultural value is not thereby diminished.

23. Any work done on the cultural heritage should aim at preserving its traditional appearance, and protecting it from any new construction or remodelling which might impair the relations of mass or colour between it and its surroundings.

24. The harmony established by time and man between a monument and its surroundings is of the greatest importance and should not, as a general rule, be disturbed or destroyed. The isolation of a monument by demolishing its surroundings should not, as a general rule, be authorized; nor should the moving of a monument be contemplated save as an exceptional means of dealing with a problem, justified by pressing considerations.

25. Member States should take measures to protect their cultural and natural heritage against the possible harmful effects of the technological developments characteristic of modern civilization. Such measures should be designed to counter the effects of shocks and vibrations caused by machines and vehicles. Measures should also be taken to prevent pollution and guard against natural disasters and calamities, and to provide for the repair of damage to the cultural and natural heritage.

26. Since the circumstances governing the rehabilitation of groups of buildings are not everywhere identical, Member States should provide for a social science inquiry in appropriate cases, in order to ascertain precisely what are the social and cultural needs of the community in which the group of buildings concerned is situated. Any rehabilitation operation should pay special attention to enabling man to work, to develop and to achieve fulfilment in the restored setting.

27. Member States should undertake studies and research on the geology and ecology of items of the natural heritage, such as park, wildlife, refuge or recreation areas, or other equivalent reserves, in order to appreciate their scientific value, to determine the impact of visitor use and to monitor interrelationships so as to avoid serious damage to the heritage and to provide adequate background for the management of the fauna and flora.

28. Member States should keep abreast of advances in transportation, communication, audio-visual techniques, automatic data-processing and other appropriate technology, and of cultural and recreational trends, so that the best possible facilities and services can be provided for scientific study and the enjoyment of the public, appropriate to the purpose of each area, without deterioration of the natural resources.

IV.B.6

Administrative measures

29. Each Member State should draw up, as soon as possible, an inventory for the protection of its cultural and natural heritage, including items which, without being of outstanding importance, are inseparable from their environment and contribute to its character.

30. The information obtained by such surveys of the cultural and natural heritage should be collected in a suitable form and regularly brought up to date.

31. To ensure that the cultural and natural heritage is effectively recognized at all levels of planning, Member States should prepare maps and the fullest possible documentation covering the cultural and natural property in question.

32. Member States should give thought to finding suitable uses for groups of historic buildings no longer serving their original purpose.

33. A plan should be prepared for the protection, conservation, presentation and rehabilitation of groups of buildings of historic and artistic interest. It should include peripheral protection belts, lay down the conditions for land use, and specify the buildings to be preserved and the conditions for their preservation. This plan should be incorporated into the overall town and country planning policy for the areas concerned.

34. Rehabilitation plans should specify the uses to which historic buildings are to be put, and the links there are to be between the rehabilitation area and the surrounding urban development. When the designation of a rehabilitation area is under consideration, the local authorities and representatives of the residents of the area should be consulted.

35. Any work that might result in changing the existing state of the buildings in a protected area should be subject to prior authorization by the town and country planning authorities, on the advice of the specialized services responsible for the protection of the cultural and natural heritage.

36. Internal alterations to groups of buildings and the installation of modern conveniences should be allowed if they are needed for the well-being of their occupants and provided they do not drastically alter the real characteristic features of ancient dwellings.

37. Member States should develop short- and long-range plans, based on inventories of their natural heritage, to achieve a system of conservation to meet the needs of their countries.

38. Member States should provide an advisory service to guide non-governmental organizations and owners of land on national conservation policies consistent with the productive use of the land.

39. Member States should develop policies and programmes for restoration of natural areas made derelict by industry, or otherwise despoiled by man's activities.

Legal measures

40. Depending upon their importance, the components of the cultural and natural heritage should be protected, individually or collectively, by legislation or regulations in conformity with the competence and the legal procedures of each country.

41. Measures for protection should be supplemented to the extent necessary by new provisions to promote the conservation of the cultural or natural heritage and to facilitate the presentation of its components. To that end, enforcement of protective measures should apply to individual owners and to public authorities when they are the owners of components of the cultural and natural heritage.

42. No new building should be erected, and no demolition, transformation, modification or deforestation carried out, on any property situated on or in the vicinity of a protected site, if it is likely to affect its appearance, without authorization by the specialized services.

43. Planning legislation to permit industrial development, or public and private works should take into account existing legislation on conservation. The authorities responsible for the protection of the cultural and natural heritage might take steps to expedite the necessary conservation work, either by making financial assistance available to the owner, or by acting in the owner's place and exercising their powers to have the work done, with the possibility of their obtaining reimbursement of that share of the costs which the owner would normally have paid.

44. Where required for the preservation of the property, the public authorities might be empowered to expropriate a protected building or natural site subject to the terms and conditions of domestic legislation.

45. Member States should establish regulations to control bill-posting, neon signs and other kinds of advertisement, commercial signs, camping, the erection of poles, pylons and electricity or telephone cables, the placing of television aerials, all types of vehicular traffic and parking, the placing of indicator panels, street furniture, etc., and, in general, everything connected with the equipment or occupation of property forming part of the cultural and natural heritage.

46. The effects of the measures taken to protect any element of the cultural or natural heritage should continue regardless of changes of ownership. If a protected building or natural site is sold, the purchaser should be informed that it is under protection.

47. Penalties or administrative sanctions should be applicable, in accordance with the laws and constitutional competence of each State, to anyone who wilfully destroys, mutilates or defaces a protected monument, group of buildings or site, or one which is of archaeological, historical or artistic interest. In addition, equipment used in illicit excavation might be subject to confiscation.

48. Penalties or administrative sanctions should be imposed upon those responsible for any other action detrimental to the protection, conservation or presentation of a protected component of the cultural or natural heritage, and should include provision for the restoration of an affected site to its original state in accordance with established scientific and technical standards.

Financial measures

49. Central and local authorities should, as far as possible, appropriate, in their budgets, a certain percentage of funds, proportionate to the importance of the protected property forming part of their cultural or natural heritage, for the purposes of maintaining, conserving and presenting protected property of which they are the owners, and of contributing financially to such work carried out on other protected property by the owners, whether public bodies or private persons.

50. The expenditure incurred in protecting, conserving and presenting items of the privately owned cultural and natural heritage should, so far as possible, be borne by their owners or users.

51. Tax concessions on such expenditures, or grants or loans on favourable terms, could be granted to private owners of protected properties, on condition

that they carry out work for the protection, conservation, presentation and rehabilitation of their properties in accordance with approved standards.

52. Consideration should be given to indemnifying, if necessary, owners of protected cultural and natural areas for losses they might suffer as a consequence of protective programmes.

53. The financial advantages accorded to private owners should, where appropriate, be dependent on their observance of certain conditions laid down for the benefit of the public, such as their allowing access to parks, gardens and sites, tours through all of parts of natural sites, monuments or groups of buildings, the taking of photographs, etc.

54. Special funds should be set aside in the budgets of public authorities for the protection of the cultural and natural heritage endangered by large-scale public or private works.

55. To increase the financial resources available to them, Member States may set up one or more 'Cultural and Natural Heritage Funds', as legally established public agencies, entitled to receive private gifts, donations and bequests, particularly from industrial and commercial firms.

56. Tax concessions could also be granted to those making gifts, donations or bequests for the acquisition, restoration or maintenance of specific components of the cultural and natural heritage.

57. In order to facilitate operations for rehabilitation of the natural and cultural heritage, Member States might make special arrangements, particularly by way of loans for renovation and restoration work, and might also make the necessary regulations to avoid price rises caused by real-estate speculation in the areas under consideration.

58. To avoid hardship to the poorer inhabitants consequent on their having to move from rehabilitated buildings or groups of buildings, compensation for rises in rent might be contemplated so as to enable them to keep their accommodation. Such compensation should be temporary and determined on the basis of the income of the parties concerned, so as to enable them to meet the increased costs occasioned by the work carried out.

59. Member States might facilitate the financing of work of any description for the benefit of the cultural and natural heritage, by instituting 'Loan Funds', supported by public institutions and private credit establishments,

which would be responsible for granting loans to owners at low interest rates and with repayment spread out over a long period.

VI. Educational and cultural action

60. Universities, educational establishments at all levels and life-long education establishments should organize regular courses, lectures, seminars, etc., on the history of art, architecture, the environment and town planning.

61. Member States should undertake educational campaigns to arouse widespread public interest in, and respect for, the cultural and natural heritage. Continuing efforts should be made to inform the public about what is being and can be done to protect the cultural or natural heritage and to inculcate appreciation and respect for the values it enshrines. For this purpose, all media of information should be employed as required.

62. Without overlooking the great economic and social value of the cultural and natural heritage, measures should be taken to promote and reinforce the eminent cultural and educational value of that heritage, furnishing as it does the fundamental motive for protecting, conserving and presenting it.

63. All efforts on behalf of components of the cultural and natural heritage should take account of the cultural and educational value inherent in them as representative of an environment, a form of architecture or urban design commensurate with man and on his scale.

64. Voluntary organizations should be set up to encourage national and local authorities to make full use of their powers with regard to protection, to afford them support and, if necessary, to obtain funds for them; these bodies should keep in touch with local historical societies, amenity improvement societies, local development committees and agencies concerned with tourism, etc., and might also organize visits to, and guided tours of, different items of the cultural and natural heritage for their members.

65. Information centres, museums or exhibitions might be set up to explain the work being carried out on components of the cultural and natural heritage scheduled for rehabilitation.

VII. International co-operation

66. Member States should co-operate with regard to the protection, conservation and presentation of the cultural and natural heritage, seeking aid, if it

seems desirable, from international organizations, both intergovernmental and non-governmental. Such multilateral or bilateral co-operation should be carefully co-ordinated and should take the form of measures such as the following:
(a) exchange of information and of scientific and technical publications;
(b) organization of seminars and working parties on particular subjects;
(c) provision of study and travel fellowships, and of scientific, technical and administrative staff, and equipment;
(d) provision of facilities for scientific and technical training abroad, by allowing young research workers and technicians to take part in architectural projects, archaeological excavations and the conservation of natural sites;
(e) co-ordination, within a group of Member States, of large-scale projects involving conservation, excavations, restoration and rehabilitation work, with the object of making the experience gained generally available.

The foregoing is the authentic text of the Recommendation duly adopted by the General Conference of the United Nations Educational, Scientific and Cultural Organization during its seventeenth session, which was held in Paris and declared closed the twenty-first day of November 1972.

IN FAITH WHEREOF we have appended our signatures this twenty-third day of November 1972.

The President of the General Conference   *The Director-General*

Recommendation concerning the International Exchange of Cultural Property [1]

Introduction

This recommendation is the outcome of the desire to promote greater mutual knowledge and understanding among nations, in keeping with Unesco's Constitution, by enabling their peoples to have access to each other's achievements in the various fields of culture.

Since the two instruments adopted by Unesco in 1964 and 1970 to prevent illicit trading in cultural property may have too restrictive an effect on the circulatory of cultural property, this recommendation invites Member States to develop the lawful circulation of exhibits among museums and other cultural institutions in various countries through exchanges or loans or, in the case of items possessed by a nation in many copies, through definitive assignment.

All necessary guarantees should be provided in connection with these transfers, particularly regarding the protection of items during transport and the coverage of the risks to which objects on loan are exposed.

In addition, extensive information and encouragement should be provided by Member States in order to draw the attention of cultural institutions and competent authorities in the various countries to the importance, for a better understanding among peoples, of developing all forms of lawful circulation of cultural property.

---

1. Adopted on 26 November 1976 by the General Conference of Unesco at its nineteenth session, held in Nairobi.

United Nations Educational, Scientific and
Cultural Organization

Recommendation concerning the International Exchange of Cultural Property

Adopted by the General Conference at its
nineteenth session, Nairobi, 26 November 1976

The General Conference of the United Nations Educational, Scientific and Cultural Organization, meeting in Nairobi from 26 October to 30 November 1976, at its nineteenth session,

Recalling that cultural property constitutes a basic element of civilization and national culture,

Considering that the extension and promotion of cultural exchanges directed towards a fuller mutual knowledge of achievements in various fields of culture, will contribute to the enrichment of the cultures involved, with due appreciation of the distinctive character of each and of the value of the cultures of other nations making up the cultural heritage of all mankind,

Considering that the circulation of cultural property, when regulated by legal, scientific and technical conditions calculated to prevent illicit trading in and damage to such property, is a powerful means of promoting mutual understanding and appreciation among nations,

Considering that the international circulation of cultural property is still largely dependent on the activities of self-seeking parties and so tends to lead to speculation which causes the price of such property to rise, making it inaccessible to poorer countries and institutions while at the same time encouraging the spread of illicit trading,

Considering that, even when the motives behind the international circulation of this property are disinterested, the action taken usually results in unilateral services, such as short-term loans, deposits under medium- or long-term arrangements, or donations,

Considering that such unilateral operations are still limited in number and restricted in range, both because of their cost and because of the variety of complexity of the relevant regulations and practices,

Considering that, while it is highly desirable to encourage such operations, by reducing or removing the obstacles to their extension, it is also vitally important to promote operations based on mutual confidence which would enable all institutions to deal with each other on an equal footing,

Considering that many cultural institutions, whatever their financial resources, possess several identical or similar specimens of cultural objects of indisputable quality and origin which are amply documented, and that some of these items, which are of only minor or secondary importance for these institutions because of their plurality, would be welcomed as valuable accessions by institutions in other countries,

Considering that a systematic policy of exchanges among cultural institutions, by which each would part with its surplus items in return for objects that it lacked, would not only be enriching to all parties but would also lead to a better use of the international community's cultural heritage which is the sum of all the national heritages,

Recalling that this policy of exchanges has already been recommended in various international agreements concluded as a result of Unesco's work,

Noting that, on these points, the effects of the above-mentioned instruments have remained limited, and that, generally speaking, the practice of exchanges between disinterested cultural institutions is not widespread, while such operations as do take place are frequently confidential or unpublicized,

Considering that it is consequently necessary to develop simultaneously not only the unilateral operations of loans, deposits or donations but also bi- or multilateral exchanges,

Having before it proposals concerning the international exchange of cultural property which appears on the agenda of the session as item 26,

Having decided, at its eighteenth session, that this question should take the form of a Recommendation to Member States,

Adopts, this twenty-sixth day of November 1976, the present Recommendation.

The General Conference recommends that Member States should apply the following provisions by taking whatever legislative or other steps may be required in conformity with the constitutional system or practice of each State, to give effect within their respective territories to the principles formulated in this Recommendation.

The General Conference recommends that Member States should bring this Recommendation to the attention of the appropriate authorities and bodies.

The General Conference recommends that Member States should submit to it, by dates and in the form to be decided upon by the Conference, reports concerning the action taken by them in pursuance of this Recommendation.

I. Definitions

1. For the purposes of this Recommendation:

'cultural institution' shall be taken to mean any permanent establishment administered in the general interest for the purpose of preserving, studying and enhancing cultural property and making it accessible to the public and which is licensed or approved by the competent public authorities of each State;

'cultural property' shall be taken to mean items which are the expression and testimony of human creation and of the evolution of nature which, in the opinion of the competent bodies in individual States, are, or may be, of historical, artistic, scientific or technical value and interest, including items in the following categories:

(a) zoological, botanical and geological specimens;
(b) archaeological objects;
(c) objects and documentation of ethnological interest;
(d) works of fine art and of the applied arts;
(e) literary, musical, photographic and cinematographic works;
(f) archives and documents;

'international exchange' shall be taken to mean any transfer of ownership, use or custody of cultural property between States or cultural institutions in different countries—whether it takes the form of the loan, deposit, sale or donation of such property—carried out under such conditions as may be agreed between the parties concerned.

II. Measures recommended

2. Bearing in mind that all cultural property forms part of the common cultural heritage of mankind and that every State has a responsibility in this respect, not only towards its own nationals but also towards the international community as a whole, Member States should adopt within the sphere of their competence, the following measures to develop the circulation of cultural property among cultural institutions in different countries in co-operation with regional and local authorities as may be required.

3. Member States, in accordance with the legislation and the constitutional system or practice and the particular circumstances of their respective countries, should adapt existing statutes or regulations or adopt new legisla-

tion or regulations regarding inheritance, taxation and customs duties and take all other necessary measures in order to make it possible or easier to carry out the following operations solely for the purposes of international exchanges of cultural property between cultural institutions:

(a) definitive or temporary import or export as well as transit of cultural property;

(b) transfer of ownership or derestriction of cultural property belonging to a public body or a cultural institution.

4. Member States should foster, if they deem it advisable, the establishment either under their direct authority or through cultural institutions of files of requests for and offers of exhanges of cultural property made available for international exchange.

5. Offers of exchange should be entered in the files only when it has been established that the legal status of the items concerned conforms to national law and that the offering institution has legal title for this purpose.

6. Offers of exchanges should include full scientific, technical and, if requested, legal documentation calculated to ensure the most favourable conditions for the cultural utilization, the conservation and, where appropriate, the restoration of the items in question.

7. Exchange agreements should include an indication that the recipient institution is prepared to take all necessary measures of conservation for the proper protection of the cultural property involved.

8. Consideration should be given to the granting of additional financial assistance to cultural institutions, or to the setting aside of part of the existing levels of financial assistance, to facilitate the carrying out of international exchanges.

9. Member States should give special attention to the problem of covering the risks to which cultural property is exposed throughout the duration of loans, including the period spent in transport, and should, in particular, study the possibility of introducing government guarantee and compensation systems for the loan of objects of great value, such as those which already exist in certain countries.

10. Member States, in accordance with their constitutional practice, should examine the possibility of entrusting to appropriate specialized bodies the task of co-ordinating the various operations involved in the international exchange of cultural property.

III. International co-operation

11. With the assistance of all competent organizations, whether regional, national or international, intergovernmental or non-governmental, and in accordance with their constitutional practice, Member States should launch an extensive campaign of information and encouragement aimed at cultural institutions in all countries and at the professional staff of all categories—administrative, academic and scientific—who are in charge of the national cultural property, at the national or regional level, drawing their attention to the important contribution which can be made to the promotion of a better mutual understanding of all peoples by developing all forms of international circulation of cultural property and encouraging them to participate in such exchanges.

12. This campaign should cover the following points in particular:
(1) cultural institutions having already concluded agreements on the international circulation of cultural property should be invited to publicize all provisions which are of a general nature and could thus serve as a model, but not provisions of a special nature such as the description of the particular items in question, their evaluation or other specific technical details;
(2) the competent specialized organizations, and particularly the International Council of Museums, should produce or enlarge one or more practical handbooks describing every possible form of circulation of cultural property and emphasizing their specific features. These handbooks should include model contracts, including insurance contracts, for every possible type of agreement. With the help of the competent national authorities, the handbooks should be widely distributed to all the professional organizations involved in the various countries;
(3) in order to facilitate the preparatory studies for the conclusion of exchange agreements, the following should be widely distributed in all countries:
    (a) various publications (books, periodicals, museum and exhibition catalogues, photographic documentation) produced in all countries by institutions which are custodians of cultural property;
    (b) the files of exchange offers and requests compiled in each country;
(4) the attention of cultural institutions in all countries should be drawn especially to the opportunities for reassembling a presently dismembered work which would be afforded by a system of successive loans, without transfer of ownership, enabling each of the holding institutions to take its turn to display the work in its entirety.

13. Should the parties to an international exchange of cultural property encounter technical difficulties in carrying out such an exchange they may re-

quest the opinion of one or more experts nominated by them after consultation with the Director-General of Unesco.

IV. Federal States

14. In giving effect to the present Recommendation, Member States which have a federal or non-unitary constitutional system might follow the principles set forth in Article 34 of the Convention concerning the Protection of the World Cultural and Natural Heritage, adopted by the General Conference at its seventeenth session.

V. Action against illicit trading in cultural property

15. The development of international exchanges should enable the cultural institutions of the different Member States to enlarge their collections by acquiring cultural property of lawful origin, accompanied by documentation calculated to bring out their full cultural significance. Accordingly, Member States should take all necessary steps, with the help of the international organizations concerned, to ensure that the development of such exchanges goes hand in hand with an extension of the action taken against every possible form of illicit trading in cultural property.

The foregoing is the authentic text of the Recommendation duly adopted by the General Conference of the United Nations Educational, Scientific and Cultural Organization during its nineteenth session, which was held in Nairobi and declared closed the thirtieth day of November 1976.

IN FAITH WHEREOF we have appended our signatures.

The President of the General Conference   *The Director-General*

Recommendation concerning the Safeguarding and Contemporary Role of Historic Areas [1]

Introduction

In view of the real dangers of uniformity and depersonalization of housing that modern town planning entails throughout the world, the survival of historic areas is of capital importance to every people seeking to preserve their true cultural dimension and their individuality. Because of the constant aggravation of damage to old centres and districts of towns, and to traditional villages, and because the preservation and the effective presentation of such areas raise complex problems, a recommendation dealing specifically with this matter was deemed necessary.

This Recommendation invites Member States to adopt an overall safeguarding policy, applicable throughout their territory, for preserving historic areas, and lays down the various measures which should be taken.

On the legal and administrative side, a specific system for the protection of historic areas should be instituted, and statutory provisions regarding town planning, housing and regional planning should be harmonized with those concerning the safeguarding of the architectural heritage.

As to the technical aspect, all areas to be protected should be listed forthwith, and complete analytical inventories should be drawn up for each area, incorporating the architectural, economic and social data needed for the programming of safeguarding operations. Safeguarding programmes should include revitalization designed to maintain commerce and crafts in historic areas and to develop cultural activities in them.

On the social side, the public authorities should ensure that the people con-

1. Adopted on 26 November 1976 by the General Conference of Unesco at its nineteenth session, held in Nairobi.

cerned are closely associated with the planning and implementation of safeguarding operations. For this purpose, advisory groups of inhabitants and owners should be set up to work in conjunction with decision-making and management bodies. Care should also be taken to ensure that the renovation of old buildings and districts does not lead to changes in the pattern of residence causing hardship to the least privileged social categories. The public should be kept regularly informed of the objectives of safeguarding plans and of ways in which they are carried out.

United Nations Educational, Scientific and
Cultural Organization

Recommendation concerning the Safeguarding and Contemporary Role of Historic Areas

Adopted by the General Conference at its
nineteenth session, Nairobi, 26 November 1976

The General Conference of the United Nations Educational, Scientific and Cultural Organization, meeting in Nairobi at its nineteenth session, from 26 October to 30 November 1976,

Considering that historic areas are part of the daily environment of human beings everywhere, that they represent the living presence of the past which formed them, that they provide the variety in life's background needed to match the diversity of society, and that by so doing they gain in value and acquire an additional human dimension,

Considering that historic areas afford down the ages the most tangible evidence of the wealth and diversity of cultural, religious and social activities and that their safeguarding and their integration into the life of contemporary society is a basic factor in town-planning and land development,

Considering that in face of the dangers of stereotyping and depersonalization, this living evidence of days gone by is of vital importance for humanity and for nations who find in it both the expression of their way of life and one of the corner-stones of their identity,

Noting that throughout the world, under the pretext of expansion or modernization, demolition ignorant of what it is demolishing and irrational and inappropriate reconstruction work is causing serious damage to this historic heritage,

Considering that historic areas are an immovable heritage whose destruction may often lead to social disturbance, even where it does not lead to economic loss,

Considering that this situation entails responsibilities for every citizen and lays on public authorities obligations which they alone are capable of fulfilling,

IV.B.9

Considering that in order to save these irreplaceable assets from the dangers of deterioration or even total destruction to which they are thus exposed, it is for each State to adopt, as a matter of urgency, comprehensive and energetic policies for the protection and revitalization of historic areas and their surroundings as part of national, regional or local planning,

Noting the absence in many cases of a legislation effective and flexible enough concerning the architectural heritage and its interconnexion with town-planning, territorial, regional or local planning,

Noting that the General Conference has already adopted international instruments for the protection of the cultural and natural heritage such as the Recommendation on International Principles Applicable to Archaeological Excavations (1956), the Recommendation Concerning the Safeguarding of the Beauty and Character of Landscapes and Sites (1962), the Recommendation Concerning the Preservation of Cultural Property Endangered by Public or Private Works (1968), and the Recommendation Concerning the Protection, at National Level, of the Cultural and Natural Heritage (1972),

Desiring to supplement and extend the application of the standards and principles laid down in these international instruments,

Having before it proposals concerning the safeguarding and contemporary rôle of historic areas, which question appears on the agenda of the session as item 27,

Having decided at its eighteenth session that this question should take the form of a Recommendation to Member States,

Adopts, this twenty-sixth day of November 1976, the present Recommendation.

The General Conference recommends that Member States apply the above provisions by adopting, as a national law or in some other form, measures with a view to giving effect to the principles and norms set out in this Recommendation in the territories under their jurisdiction.

The General Conference recommends that Member States bring this Recommendation to the attention of the national, regional and local authorities and of institutions, services or bodies and associations concerned with the safeguarding of historic areas and their environment.

The General Conference recommends that Member States report to it, at the dates and in the form determined by it, on action taken by them on this Recommendation.

I. Definitions

1. For the purposes of the present recommendation:
(a) 'Historic and architectural (including vernacular) areas' shall be taken to mean any groups of buildings, structures and open spaces including archaeological and palaeontological sites, constituting human settlements in an urban or rural environment, the cohesion and value of which, from the archaeological, architectural, prehistoric, historic, aesthetic or sociocultural point of view are recognized.

Among these 'areas', which are very varied in nature, it is possible to distinguish the following in particular: prehistoric sites, historic towns, old urban quarters, villages and hamlets as well as homogeneous monumental groups, it being understood that the latter should as a rule be carefully preserved unchanged.
(b) The 'environment' shall be taken to mean the natural or man-made setting which influences the static or dynamic way these areas are perceived or which is directly linked to them in space or by social, economic or cultural ties.
(c) 'Safeguarding' shall be taken to mean the identification, protection, conservation, restoration, renovation, maintenance and revitalization of historic or traditional areas and their environment.

II. General principles

2. Historic areas and their surroundings should be regarded as forming an irreplaceable universal heritage. The governments and the citizens of the States in whose territory they are situated should deem it their duty to safeguard this heritage and integrate it into the social life of our times. The national, regional or local authorities should be answerable for their performance of this duty in the interests of all citizens and of the international community, in accordance with the conditions of each Member State as regards the allocation of powers.

3. Every historic area and its surroundings should be considered in their totality as a coherent whole whose balance and specific nature depend on the fusion of the parts of which it is composed and which include human activities as much as the buildings, the spatial organization and the surroundings. All valid elements, including human activities, however modest, thus have a significance in relation to the whole which must not be disregarded.

4. Historic areas and their surroundings should be actively protected against damage of all kinds, particularly that resulting from unsuitable use, unneces-

IV.B.9

sary additions and misguided or insensitive changes such as will impair their authenticity, and from damage due to any form of pollution. Any restoration work undertaken should be based on scientific principles. Similarly, great attention should be paid to the harmony and aesthetic feeling produced by the linking or the contrasting of the various parts which make up the groups of buildings and which give to each group its particular character.

5. In the conditions of modern urbanization, which leads to a considerable increase in the scale and density of buildings, apart from the danger of direct destruction of historic areas, there is a real danger that newly developed areas can ruin the environment and character of adjoining historic areas. Architects and town-planners should be careful to ensure that views from and to monuments and historic areas are not spoilt and that historic areas are integrated harmoniously into contemporary life.

6. At a time when there is a danger that a growing universality of building techniques and architectural forms may create a uniform environment throughout the world, the preservation of historic areas can make an outstanding contribution to maintaining and developing the cultural and social values of each nation. This can contribute to the architectural enrichment of the cultural heritage of the world.

III. National, regional and local policy

7. In each Member State a national, regional and local policy should be drawn up, in conformity with the conditions of each State as regards the allocation of powers, so that legal, technical, economic and social measures may be taken by the national, regional or local authorities with a view to safeguarding historic areas and their surroundings and adapting them to the requirements of modern life. The policy thus laid down should influence planning at national, regional or local level and provide guidelines for town-planning and regional and rural development planning at all levels, the activities stemming from it forming an essential component in the formulation of aims and programmes, the assignment of responsibilities and the conduct of operations. The co-operation of individuals and private associations should be sought in implementing the safeguarding policy.

IV. Safeguarding measures

8. Historic areas and their surroundings should be safeguarded in conformity with the principles stated above and with the methods set out below, the specific measures being determined according to the legislative and constitu-

tional competence and the organizational and economic structure of each State.

Legal and administrative measures

9. The application of an overall policy for safeguarding historic areas and their surroundings should be based on principles which are valid for the whole of each country. Member States should adapt the existing provisions, or, where necessary, enact new laws and regulations, so as to secure the protection of historic areas and their surroundings taking into account the provisions contained in this chapter and in the following chapters. They should encourage the adaptation or the adoption of regional or local measures to ensure such protection. Laws concerning town and regional planning and housing policy should also be reviewed so as to co-ordinate and bring them into line with the laws concerning the safeguarding of the architectural heritage.

10. The provisions establishing a system for safeguarding historic areas should set out the general principles relating to the establishment of the necessary plans and documents and, in particular:
the general conditions and restrictions applicable to the protected areas and their surroundings;
a statement as to the programmes and operations to be planned for the purpose of conservation and provision of public services;
maintenance to be carried out and the designation of those to be responsible for it;
the fields to which town-planning, redevelopment and rural land management are applicable;
the designation of the body responsible for authorizing any restoration, modification, new construction or demolition within the protected perimeter;
the means by which the safeguarding programmes are to be financed and carried out.

11. Safeguarding plans and documents should define:
the areas and items to be protected;
the specific conditions and restrictions applicable to them;
the standards to be observed in the work of maintenance, restoration and improvements;
the general conditions governing the establishment of the supply systems and services needed in urban or rural life;
the conditions governing new constructions.

12. These laws should also in principle include provisions designed to prevent any infringement of the preservation laws, as well as any speculative rise in property values within the protected areas which could compromise protection and restoration planned in the interests of the community as a whole. These provisions could involve town-planning measures affording a means of influencing the price of building land, such as the establishment of neighbourhood or smaller development plans, granting the right of pre-emption to a public body, compulsory purchase in the interests of safeguarding or rehabilitation or automatic intervention in the case of failure to act on the part of the owners, and could provide for effective penalties such as the suspension of operations, compulsory restoration and/or a suitable fine.

13. Public authorities as well as individuals must be obliged to comply with the measures for safeguarding. However, machinery for appeal against arbitrary or unjust decisions should be provided.

14. The provisions concerning the setting up of public and private bodies and concerning public and private work projects should be adapted to the regulations governing the safeguarding of historic areas and their surroundings.

15. In particular, provisions concerning slum property and blocks and the construction of subsidized housing should be planned or amended both to fit in with the safeguarding policy and to contribute to it. The schedule of any subsidies paid should be drawn up and adjusted accordingly, in particular in order to facilitate the development of subsidized housing and public construction by rehabilitating old buildings. All demolition should in any case only concern buildings with no historic or architectural value and the subsidies involved should be carefully controlled. Further, a proportion of the funds earmarked for the construction of subsidized housing should be allocated to the rehabilitation of old buildings.

16. The legal consequences of the protection measures as far as buildings and land are concerned should be made public and should be recorded by a competent official body.

17. Making due allowance for the conditions specific to each country and the allocation of responsibilities within the various national, regional and local authorities, the following principles should underlie the operation of the safeguarding machinery:
(a) there should be an authority responsible for ensuring the permanent coordination of all those concerned, e.g. national, regional and local public services or groups of individuals;

IV.B.9

(b) safeguarding plans and documents should be drawn up, once all the necessary advance scientific studies have been carried out, by multidisciplinary
teams composed, in particular, of:
specialists in conservation and restoration, including art historians;
architects and town-planners;
sociologists and economists;
ecologists and landscape architects;
specialists in public health and social welfare;
and, more generally, all specialists in disciplines involved in the protection
and enhancement of historic areas;
(c) the authorities should take the lead in sounding the opinions and organizing the participation of the public concerned;
(d) the safeguarding plans and documents should be approved by the body
designated by law;
(e) the public authorities reponsible for giving effect to the safeguarding provisions and regulations at all levels, national, regional and local, should be
provided with the necessary staff and given adequate technical, administrative and financial resources.

Technical, economic and social measures

18. A list of historic areas and their surroundings to be protected should be
drawn up at national, regional or local level. It should indicate priorities so
that the limited resources available for protection may be allocated
judiciously. Any protection measures, of whatever nature, that need to be
taken as a matter of urgency should be taken without waiting for the safeguarding plans and documents to be prepared.

19. A survey of the area as a whole, including an analysis of its spatial evolution, should be made. It should cover archaeological, historical, architectural,
technical and economic data. An analytical document should be drawn up so
as to determine which buildings or groups of buildings are to be protected
with great care, conserved under certain conditions, or, in quite exceptional
and thoroughly documented circumstances, destroyed. This would enable the
authorities to call a halt to any work incompatible with this recommendation.
Additionally, an inventory of public and private open spaces and their vegeta-
tion should be drawn up for the same purposes.

20. In addition to this architectural survey, thorough surveys of social, economic, cultural and technical data and structures and of the wider urban or
regional context are necessary. Studies should include, if possible, demo-
graphic data and an analysis of economic, social and cultural activities, ways

of life and social relationships, land-tenure problems, the urban infrastructure, the state of the road system, communication networks and the reciprocal links between protected areas and surrounding zones. The authorities concerned should attach the greatest importance to these studies and should bear in mind that valid safeguarding plans cannot be prepared without them.

21. After the survey described above has been completed and before the safeguarding plans and specifications are drawn up, there should in principle be a programming operation in which due account is taken both of town-planning, architectural, economic and social considerations and of the ability of the urban and rural fabric to assimilate functions that are compatible with its specific character. The programming operation should aim at bringing the density of settlement to the desired level and should provide for the work to be carried out in stages as well as for the temporary accommodation needed while it is proceeding, and premises for the permanent rehousing of those inhabitants who cannot return to their previous dwellings. This programming operation should be undertaken with the closest possible participation of the communities and groups of people concerned. Because the social, economic and physical context of historic areas and their surroundings may be expected to change over time, survey and analysis should be a continuing process. It is accordingly essential that the preparation of safeguarding plans and their execution be undertaken on the basis of studies available, rather than being postponed while the planning process is refined.

22. Once the safeguarding plans and specifications have been drawn up and approved by the competent public authority, it would be desirable for them to be executed either by their authors or under their authority.

23. In historic areas containing features from several different periods, preservation should be carried out taking into account the manifestations of all such periods.

24. Where safeguarding plans exist urban development or slum clearance programmes consisting of the demolition of buildings of no architectural or historic interest and which are structurally too unsound to be kept, the removal of extensions and additional storeys of no value, and sometimes even the demolition of recent buildings which break the unity of the area, may only be authorized in conformity with the plan.

25. Urban development or slum clearance programmes for areas not covered by safeguarding plans should respect buildings and other elements of architectural or historic value as well as accompanying buildings. If such elements are

likely to be adversely affected by the programme, safeguarding plans as indicated above should be drawn up in advance of demolition.

26. Constant supervision is necessary to ensure that these operations are not conducive to excessive profits nor serve other purposes contrary to the objectives of the plan.

27. The usual security standards applicable to fire and natural catastrophes should be observed in any urban development or slum clearance programme affecting a historic area, provided that this be compatible with the criteria applicable to the preservation of the cultural heritage. If conflict does occur, special solutions should be sought, with the collaboration of all the services concerned, so as to provide the maximum security, while not impairing the cultural heritage.

28. Particular care should be devoted to regulations for and control over new buildings so as to ensure that their architecture adapts harmoniously to the spatial organization and setting of the groups of historic buildings. To this end, an analysis of the urban context should precede any new construction not only so as to define the general character of the group of buildings but also to analyse its dominant features, e.g. the harmony of heights, colours, materials and forms, constants in the way the façades and roofs are built, the relationship between the volume of buildings and the spatial volume, as well as their average proportions and their position. Particular attention should be given to the size of the lots since there is a danger that any reorganization of the lots may cause a change of mass which could be deleterious to the harmony of the whole.

29. The isolation of a monument through the demolition of its surroundings should not generally be authorized, neither should a monument be moved unless in exceptional circumstances and for unavoidable reasons.

30. Historic areas and their surroundings should be protected from the disfigurement caused by the erection of poles, pylons and electricity or telephone cables and the placing of television aerials and large-scale advertising signs. Where these already exist appropriate measures should be taken for their removal. Bill-posting, neon signs and other kinds of advertisement, commercial signs, street pavements and furniture, should be planned with the greatest care and controlled so that they fit harmoniously into the whole. Special efforts should be made to prevent all forms of vandalism.

IV.B.9

31. Member States and groups concerned should protect historic areas and their surroundings against the increasingly serious environmental damage caused by certain technological developments—in particular the various forms of pollution—by banning harmful industries in the proximity of these areas and by taking preventive measures to counter the destructive effects of noise, shocks and vibrations caused by machines and vehicles. Provision should further be made for measures to counter the harm resulting from over-exploitation by tourism.

32. Member States should encourage and assist local authorities to seek solutions to the conflict existing in most historic groupings between motor traffic on the one hand and the scale of the buildings and their architectural qualities on the other. To solve the conflict and to encourage pedestrian traffic, careful attention should be paid to the placing of, and access to, peripheral and even central car parks and routing systems established which will facilitate pedestrian traffic, service access and public transport alike. Many rehabilitation operations such as putting electricity and other cables underground, too expensive if carried out singly, could then be co-ordinated easily and economically with the development of the road system.

33. Protection and restoration should be accompanied by revitalization activities. It would thus be essential to maintain appropriate existing functions, in particular trades and crafts, and establish new ones, which, if they are to be viable, in the long term, should be compatible with the economic and social context of the town, region or country where they are introduced. The cost of safeguarding operations should be evaluated not only in terms of the cultural value of the buildings but also in relation to the value they acquire through the use made of them. The social problems of safeguarding cannot be seen correctly unless reference is made to both these value scales. These functions should answer the social, cultural and economic needs of the inhabitants without harming the specific nature of the area concerned. A cultural revitalization policy should make historic areas centres of cultural activities and give them a central rôle to play in the cultural development of the communities around them.

34. In rural areas all works which cause disturbances and all changes of economic and social structure should be carefully controlled so as to preserve the integrity of historic rural communities within their natural setting.

35. Safeguarding activities should couple the public authorities' contribution with the contribution made by the individual or collective owners and the inhabitants and users, separately or together, who should be encouraged to put forward suggestions and generally play an active part. Constant co-operation between the community and the individual should thus be established at all

levels particularly through methods such as: information adapted to the types of persons concerned; surveys adapted to the persons questioned; establishment of advisory groups attached to planning teams; representation of owners, inhabitants and users in an advisory function on bodies responsible for decision-making, management and the organization of operations connected with plans for safeguarding, or the creation of public corporations to play a part in the plan's implementation.

36. The formation of voluntary conservation groups and non-profit-making associations and the establishment of honorary or financial rewards should be encouraged so that specially meritorious work in all aspects of safeguarding may be recognized.

37. Availability of the necessary funds for the level of public investment provided for in the plans for the safeguarding of historic areas and their surroundings should be ensured by including adequate appropriations in the budgets of the central, regional and local authorities. All these funds should be centrally managed by public, private or semi-public bodies entrusted with the co-ordination of all forms of financial aid at national, regional or local level and with the channelling of them according to an overall plan of action.

38. Public assistance in the forms described below should be based on the principle that, wherever this is appropriate and necessary, the measures taken by the authorities concerned should take into account the 'extra cost' of restoration, i.e. the additional cost imposed on the owner as compared with the new market or rental value of the building.

39. In general, such public funds should be used primarily to conserve existing buildings including especially buildings for low rental housing and should not be allocated to the construction of new buildings unless the latter do not prejudice the use and functions of existing buildings.

40. Grants, subsidies, loans at favourable rates, or tax concessions should be made available to private owners and to users carrying out work provided for by the safeguarding plans and in conformity with the standards laid down in those plans. These tax concessions, grants and loans could be made first and foremost to groups of owners or users of living accommodation and commercial property, since joint operations are more economical than individual action. The financial concessions granted to private owners and users should, where appropriate, be dependent on covenants requiring the observance of certain conditions laid down in the public interest, and ensuring the integrity of the buildings such as allowing the buildings to be visited and allowing access to parks, gardens or sites, the taking of photographs, etc.

41. Special funds should be set aside in the budgets of public and private bodies for the protection of groups of historic buildings endangered by large-scale public works and pollution. Public authorities should also set aside special funds for the repair of damage caused by natural disasters.

42. In addition, all government departments and agencies active in the field of public works should arrange their programmes and budgets so as to contribute to the rehabilitation of groups of historic buildings by financing work which is both in conformity with their own aims and the aims of the safeguarding plan.

43. To increase the financial resources available to them, Member States should encourage the setting up of public and/or private financing agencies for the safeguarding of historic areas and their surroundings. These agencies should have corporate status and be empowered to receive gifts from individuals, foundations and industrial and commercial concerns. Special tax concessions may be granted to donors.

44. The financing of work of any description carried out for the safeguarding of historic areas and their surroundings by setting up a loans corporation, could be facilitated by public institutions and private credit establishments, which would be responsible for making loans to owners at reduced rates of interest with repayment spread out over a long period.

45. Member States and other levels of government concerned could facilitate the creation of non-profit-making associations responsible for buying and, where appropriate after restoration, selling buildings by using revolving funds established for the special purpose of enabling owners of historic buildings who wish to safeguard them and preserve their character to continue to reside there.

46. It is most important that safeguarding measures should not lead to a break in the social fabric. To avoid hardship to the poorest inhabitants consequent on their having to move from buildings or groups of buildings due for renovation, compensation for rises in rent could enable them to keep their homes, commercial premises and workshops and their traditional living patterns and occupations, especially rural crafts, small-scale agriculture, fishing, etc. This compensation, which would be income-related, would help those concerned to pay the increased rentals resulting from the work carried out.

V. Research education and information

47. In order to raise the standard of work of the skilled workers and craftsmen required and to encourage the whole population to realize the need for safe-

guarding and to take part in it, the following measures should be taken by Member States, in accordance with their legal and constitutional competence.

48. Member States and groups concerned should encourage the systematic study of, and research on:
town-planning aspects of historic areas and their environment;
the interconnexions between safeguarding and planning at all levels;
methods of conservation applicable to historic areas;
the alteration of materials;
the application of modern techniques to conservation work;
the crafts techniques indispensable for safeguarding.

49. Specific education concerning the above questions and including practical training periods should be introduced and developed. In addition, it is essential to encourage the training of skilled workers and craftsmen specializing in the safeguarding of historic areas, including any open spaces surrounding them. Furthermore, it is necessary to encourage the crafts themselves, which are jeopardized by the processes of industrialization. It is desirable that the institutions concerned co-operate in this matter with specialized international agencies such as the Centre for the Study of the Preservation and Restoration of Cultural Property, in Rome, the International Council of Monuments and Sites (ICOMOS) and the International Council of Museums (ICOM).

50. The education of administrative staff for the needs of local development in the field of safeguarding of historic areas should be financed where applicable and needed and directed by the appropriate authorities according to a long-term programme.

51. Awareness of the need for safeguarding work should be encouraged by education in school, out of school and at university and by using information media such as books, the press, television, radio, cinema and travelling exhibitions. Clear, comprehensive information should be provided as to the advantages—not only aesthetic, but also social and economic—to be reaped from a well-conducted policy for the safeguarding of historic areas and their surroundings. Such information should be widely circulated among specialized private and government bodies and the general public so that they may know why and how their surroundings can be improved in this way.

52. The study of historic areas should be included in education at all levels, especially in history teaching, so as to inculcate in young minds an understanding of and respect for the works of the past and to demonstrate the rôle of this heritage in modern life. Education of this kind should make wide use of audio-visual media and of visits to groups of historic buildings.

53. Refresher courses for teachers and guides and the training of instructors should be facilitated so as to aid groups of young people and adults wishing to learn about historic areas.

VI. International co-operation

54. Member States should co-operate with regard to the safeguarding of historic areas and their surroundings, seeking aid, if it seems desirable, from international organizations, both intergovernmental and non-governmental, in particular that of the Unesco-ICOM-ICOMOS Documentation Centre. Such multilateral or bilateral co-operation should be carefully co-ordinated and should take the form of measures such as the following:
(a) exchange of information in all forms and of scientific and technical publications;
(b) organization of seminars and working parties on particular subjects;
(c) provision of study and travel fellowships, and the dispatch of scientific, technical and administrative staff, and equipment;
(d) joint action to combat pollution of all kinds;
(e) implementation of large-scale conservation, restoration and rehabilitation projects for historic areas and publication of the experience acquired. In frontier areas where the task of developing and safeguarding historic areas and their surroundings gives rise to problems jointly affecting Member States on either side of the frontier, they should co-ordinate their policies and activities to ensure that the cultural heritage is used and protected in the best possible way;
(f) mutual assistance between neighbouring countries for the preservation of areas of common interest characteristic of the historic and cultural development of the region.

55. In conformity with the spirit and the principles of this recommendation, a Member State should not take any action to demolish or change the character of the historic quarters, towns and sites, situated in territories occupied by that State.

The foregoing is the authentic text of the Recommendation duly adopted by the General Conference of the United Nations Educational, Scientific and Cultural Organization during its nineteenth session, which was held in Nairobi and declared closed the thirtieth day of November 1976.

IN FAITH WHEREOF we have appended our signatures.

The President of the General Conference   *The Director-General*

Recommendation for the Protection of Movable Cultural Property[1]

Introduction

The increase in the number of thefts, acts of vandalism, illegal excavations and illicit exports of cultural property, coupled with the risk of damage to which works of art are at present exposed by temporary exhibitions, owing to the frequency of movements and the large number of visitors, has become a subject of serious concern to all those with responsibility for the safeguarding of such property. Furthermore, as a result of the greater risks involved and the increase in the commercial value of cultural property, the cost of insurance has become so high as to be beyond the means of most museums, and is a serious obstacle to the organization of international exhibitions.

Ways of reducing the risks and the cost of covering them exist, but they need to be applied more resolutely and in a co-ordinated manner. It was for this purpose that the General Conference of Unesco adopted this Recommendation, which proposes that Member States adopt a series of measures aimed, in particular, at the improvement of security systems in museums and similar institutions, better protection for private collections, religious buildings and archaeological sites, risk prevention during transport and temporary exhibitions, and the punishment for offences involving cultural property, such as theft, illegal excavations and acts of vandalism. The Recommendation also advocates the adoption by museums or similar institutions of a programme of risk-management in order to obtain the best possible insurance conditions in terms of coverage and cost, together with the institution of a system of total or partial government guarantees

---

1. Adopted on 28 November 1978 by the General Conference of Unesco at its twentieth session, held in Paris.

IV.B.10.Intro.1

to cover risks in the case of temporary exhibitions or other loans of cultural items granted for cultural purposes.

United Nations Educational, Scientific and
Cultural Organization

Recommendation for the Protection of Movable Cultural Property

Adopted by the General Conference at its
twentieth session, Paris, 28 November 1978

The General Conference of the United Nations Educational, Scientific and Cultural Organization, meeting in Paris from 24 October to 28 November 1978, at its twentieth session,

Noting the great interest in cultural property now finding expression throughout the world in the creation of numerous museums and similar institutions, the growing number of exhibitions, the constantly increasing flow of visitors to collections, monuments and archaeological sites, and the intensification of cultural exchanges,

Considering that this is a very positive development which should be encouraged, in particular by applying the measures advocated in the Recommendation concerning the International Exchange of Cultural Property adopted by the General Conference at its nineteenth session in 1976,

Considering that the growing desire of the public to know and appreciate the wealth of the cultural heritage, of whatever origin, has nevertheless led to an increase in all the dangers to which cultural property is exposed as a result of particularly easy access or inadequate protection, the risks inherent in transport, and the recrudescence, in some countries, of clandestine excavation, thefts, illicit traffic and acts of vandalism,

Noting that because of this aggravation of the risks, but also as a consequence of the increase in the market value of cultural items, the cost of comprehensive insurance in countries where there is no adequate system of governmental guarantees is beyond the means of most museums and is a definite impediment to the organization of international exhibitions and other exchanges between different countries,

Considering that movable cultural property representing the different cultures forms part of the common heritage of mankind and that every State is

IV.B.10

therefore morally responsible to the international community as a whole for its safeguarding,

Considering that States should accordingly intensify and give general effect to such measures for the prevention and management of risks as will ensure the effective protection of movable cultural property and, at the same time, reduce the cost of covering the risks incurred,

Wishing to supplement and extend the scope of the norms and principles laid down in this respect by the General Conference, in particular in the Convention for the Protection of Cultural Property in the Event of Armed Conflict (1954), the Recommendation on International Principles Applicable to Archaeological Excavation (1956), the Recommendation on the Most Effective Means of Rendering Museums Accessible to Everyone (1960), the Recommendation on the Means of Prohibiting and Preventing the Illicit Import, Export and Transfer of Ownership of Cultural Property (1964), the Convention on the Means of Prohibiting and Preventing the Illicit Import, Export and Transfer of Ownership of Cultural Property (1970), the Recommendation concerning the Protection, at National Level, of the Cultural and Natural Heritage (1972), the Convention concerning the Protection of the World Cultural and Natural Heritage (1972) and the Recommendation concerning the International Exchange of Cultural Property (1976),

Having before it proposals concerning the protection of movable cultural property,

Having decided, at its nineteenth session, that this question should take the form of a recommendation to Member States,

Adopts, this twenty-eighth day of November 1978, the present Recommendation.

The General Conference recommends that Member States apply the following provisions by taking whatever legislative or other steps may be required, in conformity with the constitutional system or practice of each State, to give effect within their respective territories to the principles and norms formulated in this Recommendation.

The General Conference recommends that Member States bring this Recommendation to the attention of the appropriate authorities and bodies.

The General Conference recommends that Member States submit to it, by dates and in the form to be decided upon by the Conference, reports concerning the action taken by them in pursuance of this Recommendation.

I. Definitions

1. For the purposes of this Recommendation:
(a) 'movable cultural property' shall be taken to mean all movable objects which are the expression and testimony of human creation or of the evolution of nature and which are of archaeological, historical, artistic, scientific or technical value and interest, including items in the following categories:
   (i) products of archaeological exploration and excavations conducted on land and under water;
   (ii) antiquities such as tools, pottery, inscriptions, coins, seals, jewellery, weapons and funerary remains, including mummies;
   (iii) items resulting from the dismemberment of historical monuments;
   (iv) material of anthropological and ethnological interest;
   (v) items relating to history, including the history of science and technology and military and social history, to the life of peoples and national leaders, thinkers, scientists and artists and to events of national importance;
   (vi) items of artistic interest, such as:
   paintings and drawings, produced entirely by hand on any support and in any material (excluding industrial designs and manufactured articles decorated by hand);
   original prints, and posters and photographs, as the media for original creativity;
   original artistic assemblages and montages in any material;
   works of statuary art and sculpture in any material;
   works of applied art in such materials as glass, ceramics, metal, wood, etc.;
   (vii) manuscripts and incunabula, codices, books, documents or publications of special interest;
   (viii) items of numismatic (medals and coins) and philatelic interest;
   (ix) archives, including textual records, maps and other cartographic materials, photographs, cinematographic films, sound recordings and machine-readable records;
   (x) items of furniture, tapestries, carpets, dress and musical instruments;
   (xi) zoological, botanical and geological specimens;
(b) 'protection' shall be taken to mean the prevention and coverage of risks as defined below:
   (i) 'prevention of risks' means all the measures required, within a comprehensive protection system, to safeguard movable cultural property from every risk to which such property may be exposed, including those resulting from armed conflict, riots or other public disorders;
   (ii) 'risk coverage' means the guarantee of indemnification in the case of

IV.B.10

damage to, deterioration, alteration or loss of movable cultural property resulting from any risk whatsoever, including risks incurred as a result of armed conflict, riots or other public disorders whether such coverage is effected through a system of governmental guarantees and indemnities, through the partial assumption of the risks by the State under a deductible or excess loss arrangement, through commercial or national insurance or through mutual insurance arrangements.

2. Each Member State should adopt whatever criteria it deems most suitable for defining the items of movable cultural property within its territory which should be given the protection envisaged in this Recommendation by reason of their archaeological, historical, artistic, scientific or technical value.

II. General principles

3. The movable cultural property thus defined includes objects belonging either to the State or public bodies or to private bodies or individuals. Since all this property constitutes an important element of the cultural heritage of the nations concernd, the prevention and coverage of the various risks, such as damage, deterioration and loss, should be considered as a whole, even though the solutions adopted may vary from case to case.

4. The growing perils which threaten the movable cultural heritage should incite all those responsible for protecting it, in whatever capacity, to play their part: staff of national and local administrations in charge of safeguarding cultural property, administrators and curators of museums and similar institutions, private owners and those responsible for religious buildings, art and antique dealers, security experts, services responsible for the suppression of crime, customs officials and the other public authorities involved.

5. The co-operation of the public is essential for truly effective protection. The public and private bodies responsible for information and teaching should strive to instil general awareness of the importance of cultural property, the dangers to which it is exposed, and the need to safeguard it.

6. Cultural property is liable to deterioration as a result of poor conditions of storage, exhibition, transport and environment (unfavourable lighting, temperature or humidity, atmospheric pollution), which in the long run may have more serious effects than accidental damage or occasional vandalism. Suitable environmental conditions should consequently be maintained in order to ensure the material security of cultural property. The responsible specialists should include in the inventories data on the physical state of the objects and recommendations concerning the requisite environmental conditions.

7. The prevention of risks also calls for the development of conservation techniques and restoration workshops and the installation of effective protection systems in museums and other institutions possessing collections of movable cultural property. Each Member State should endeavour to ensure that the most suitable measures are taken in accordance with local circumstances.

8. Offences concerning works of art and other cultural property are increasing in some countries, most frequently being linked to fraudulent transfers across frontiers. Thefts and plunder are organized systematically and on a large scale. Acts of vandalism are also increasing. To combat these forms of criminal activity, be they of an organized nature or the action of individuals, strict control measures are necessary. Since fakes can be used for theft or the fraudulent transformation of authentic objects, measures must also be taken to prevent their circulation.

9. Protection and the prevention of risks are much more important than compensation in the event of damage or loss, since the essential purpose is to preserve the cultural heritage, not to replace by sums of money objects which are irreplaceable.

10. Because of the considerable increase in the risks resulting during transport and temporary exhibition, from environmental changes, inept handling, faulty packaging or other unfavourable conditions, adequate coverage against damage or loss is essential. The cost of risk coverage should be reduced through the rational management by museums and similar institutions of insurance contracts or by means of full or partial governmental guarantees.

III. Measures recommended

11. In accordance with the principles and norms set out above Member States should take all necessary steps, in conformity with their legislation and constitutional system, to protect movable cultural property effectively and, in the case of transport in particular, should ensure the application of the necessary measures of care and conservation and the coverage of the risks incurred.

Measures for the prevention of risks

Museums and other similar institutions
12. Member States should take all necessary steps to ensure adequate protection for cultural property in museums and similar institutions. In particular, they should:

(a) encourage the systematic inventorying and cataloguing of cultural property, with the fullest possible details and in accordance with methods specially developed for the purpose (standardized fiches, photographs —and also, if possible, colour photographs—and, as appropriate, microfilms). Such an inventory is useful when it is desired to determine damage or deterioration to cultural property. With such documentation the necessary information can be given, with all due precautions, to the national and international authorities responsible for combating thefts, illicit trading and the circulation of fakes;

(b) encourage, as appropriate, the standardized identification of movable cultural property using unobtrusive means offered by contemporary technology;

(c) urge the museums and similar institutions to reinforce the prevention of risks by a comprehensive system of practical security measures and technical installations and to ensure that all cultural property is kept, exhibited and transported in such a way as to protect it from all elements likely to damage or destroy it, including in particular heat, light, humidity, pollution, the various chemical and biological agents, vibration and shock;

(d) provide the museums and similar institutions for which they are responsible with the necessary funds for implementing the measures set out in subparagraph (c) above;

(e) take the necessary steps to ensure that all the tasks associated with the conservation of movable cultural property are carried out in accordance with the traditional techniques best suited to the particular cultural property and the most advanced scientific methods and technology; for this purpose, a suitable system for training and the vetting of professional qualifications should be established, in order to ensure that all those involved possess the required level of competence. The facilities for this should be strengthened or, if necessary, established. If appropriate, for the sake of economy, the establishment of regional conservation and restoration centres is recommended;

(f) provide suitable training for supporting staff (including security staff) and draw up guidelines for such staff, laying down standards for the performance of their duties;

(g) encourage regular training for protection, conservation and security staff;

(h) ensure that the staff of museums and similar institutions also receive the necessary training to enable them, in the event of disasters, to co-operate effectively in the rescue operations carried out by the competent public services;

(i) encourage the publication and dissemination to those responsible, if necessary in confidential form, of the latest technical and scientific information on all aspects of the protection, conservation and security of movable cultural property;

(j) issue performance standards for all security equipment for museums and public and private collections and encourage their application.

13. No effort should be spared to avoid giving in to ransom demands, so as to discourage the theft of illegal appropriation of movable cultural property carried out for that purpose. The persons or institutions concerned should consider ways and means of making this policy known.

Private collections

14. Member States should also, in conformity with their legislation and constitutional system, facilitate the protection of collections belonging to private bodies or individuals by:

(a) inviting the owners to make inventories of their collections, to communicate the inventories to the official services responsible for the protection of the cultural heritage and, if the situation requires, to grant access to the competent official curators and technicians in order to study and advise on safeguarding measures;

(b) if appropriate, providing for incentives to the owners, such as assistance for the conservation of items listed in the inventories or appropriate fiscal measures;

(c) studying the possibility of granting fiscal benefits to those who donate or bequeath cultural property to museums or similar institutions;

(d) entrusting an official body (the department responsible for museums or the police) with the organization of an advisory service for private owners on security installations and other protective measures, including fire protection.

Movable cultural property situated in religious buildings and archaeological sites

15. To ensure that movable cultural property situated in religious buildings and archaeological sites is suitably preserved and protected against theft and plunder, Member States should encourage the construction of installations for storing it and the application of special security measures. Such measures should be in proportion to the value of the property and the extent of the risks to which it is exposed. If appropriate, governments should provide technical and financial assistance for this purpose. In view of the special significance of movable cultural property situated in religious buildings, Member States and the competent authorities should endeavour to provide for the proper protection and presentation of such property where it is located.

International exchanges

16. Since movable cultural property is particularly exposed, during transport and temporary exhibition, to risks of damage which can arise from inept handling, faulty packaging, poor conditions during temporary storage or climatic changes, as well as inadequate reception arrangements, special measures of protection are required. In the case of international exchanges Member States should:

(a) take the necessary measures to ensure that appropriate conditions of protection and care during transport and exhibition as well as adequate coverage of risks are specified and agreed on between the parties concerned. Governments through whose territory the cultural property will transit should provide assistance, if so requested;

(b) encourage the institutions concerned to:

    (i)   ensure that cultural property is transported, packed and handled in accordance with the highest standards. The measures to be taken to this effect could include the determination by experts of the most appropriate form of packaging, as well as the type and timing of transport; it is recommended that, where appropriate, the responsible curator of the lending museum accompany the property during transport and certify its conditions; the institutions responsible for the shipping and packing of the objects should attach a list describing their physical appearance, and the receiving institutions should check the objects against those lists;

    (ii) take appropriate measures to prevent any direct or indirect damage which might arise from the temporary or permanent overcrowding of the exhibition premises;

    (iii) agree, where necessary, on the methods to be used for measuring, recording and regulating the degree of humidity in order to maintain the relative humidity within definite limits, and on the measures to be taken to protect light-sensitive objects (exposure to daylight, type of lamp to be used, maximum level of illumination in lux, methods used to measure and control this level);

(c) simplify the administrative formalities relating to the lawful movement of cultural property and arrange for appropriate identification of crates and other forms of packaging containing cultural property;

(d) take steps to protect cultural property in transit or temporarily imported for the purpose of cultural exchanges, and in particular facilitate rapid customs clearance in suitable premises, which should be situated close to, and if possible on, the premises of the institution concerned, and ensure that clearance is effected with all the desirable precautions; and

(e) whenever necessary, give instructions to their diplomatic and consular representatives to enable them to take effective action to accelerate customs procedures and ensure the protection of cultural property during transport.

Education and information

17. To ensure that the population as a whole becomes aware of the value of cultural property and of the need to protect it, particularly with a view to the preservation of their cultural identity, Member States should encourage the competent authorities at national, regional or local level to:
(a) provide children, young people and adults with the means of acquiring knowledge and respect for movable cultural property using all available educational and information resources for that purpose;
(b) draw the attention of the public at large by every possible means to:
    (i) the significance and importance of cultural property, but without stressing the purely commercial value of that property;
    (ii) the opportunities available to them for participating in the activities undertaken by the competent authorities in order to protect such property.

Control measures

18. To combat thefts, illegal excavations, vandalism and the use of fakes, Member States should, where the situation demands, establish or strengthen services specifically responsible for the prevention and suppression of these offences.

19. Member States should, where the situation calls for it, take the necessary measures to:
(a) provide for sanctions or any appropriate measures, whether under the penal or civil code or administrative or other measures, in the case of the theft, pillage, receiving or illegal appropriation of movable cultural property, and of damage intentionally caused to such property; these sanctions or measures should take into account the gravity of the offence;
(b) ensure better co-ordination between all services and sectors working for the prevention of offences concerning movable cultural property and organize a system of rapid dissemination of information on such offences, including information on fakes, among official bodies and the various sectors concerned, such as museum curators and art and antique dealers;
(c) ensure proper conditions for the safeguarding of movable cultural property by taking steps to counter the neglect and abandon to which it is very often exposed and which is conducive to its deterioration.

IV.B.10

20. Member States should also encourage private collectors and art and antique dealers to transmit all information concerning fakes to the official bodies mentioned in paragraph 19(b).

Measures to improve the financing of risk coverage

Governmental guarantees
21. Member States should:
(a) give special attention to the problem of covering adequately the risks to which movable cultural property is exposed during transport and temporary exhibitions;
(b) in particular, consider instituting in any legislative, statutory or other form, a system of governmental guarantees such as those which exist in certain countries, or a system of partial assumption of the risks by the State or any community concerned with a view to covering an insurance franchise deductible or an excess of loss;
(c) within the framework of such systems and in the forms mentioned above, provide for compensation to lenders in the event of damage to, or the deterioration, alteration or loss of cultural objects loaned for the purpose of exhibition in museums or similar institutions. The provisions instituting these systems should specify the conditions and procedures governing the payment of such compensation.

22. The provisions concerning governmental guarantees should not apply to cultural property which is the object of transactions for commercial purposes.

Measures at the level of museums and similar institutions
23. Member States should also urge museums and other similar institutions to apply the principles of risk management, comprising the determination, classification, assessment, control and financing of risks of all kinds.
24. The risk management programme of all institutions which have taken out insurance should include the internal drafting of a procedures manual, periodic surveys on types of risks and the probable maximum loss, analysis of contracts and rates, market studies and a competitive bidding procedure. A person or body should be specifically entrusted with risk management.

IV. International co-operation

25. Member States should:
(a) collaborate with intergovernmental and non-governmental organizations competent in regard to the prevention and coverage of risks;

(b) strengthen at international level co-operation between official bodies responsible for the suppression of thefts and illicit trading in cultural property and for the discovery of fakes, and, in particular, urge these bodies to circulate rapidly among themselves, through machinery provided for this purpose, all useful information on illegal activities;

(c) if necessary conclude international agreements for co-operation in regard to legal aid and the prevention of offences;

(d) take part in the organization of international training courses in the conservation and restoration of movable cultural property, and in risk management, and ensure that they are regularly attended by their specialized staff;

(e) establish, in collaboration with the specialized international organizations, ethical and technical standards in the fields covered by the present Recommendation and encourage the exchange of scientific and technical information, particularly on innovations relating to the protection and conservation of movable cultural property.

The foregoing is the authentic text of the Recommendation duly adopted by the General Conference of the United Nations Educational, Scientific and Cultural Organization during its twentieth session, which was held in Paris and declared closed the twenty-eighth day of November 1978.

IN FAITH WHEREOF we have appended our signatures.

The President of the General Conference   *The Director-General*

Recommendation for the Safeguarding and Preservation of Moving Images[1]

Introduction

The purpose of this Recommendation is to safeguard and preserve cinemato-graphic, television and videographic productions (referred to in the Recommendation as 'moving images') which, because of their educational, cultural, artistic, scientific and historical value, form an integral part of nations' cultural heritage. It invites every Member State to take the necessary measures to prevent the loss, unwarranted disposal or deterioration of any item of its moving image heritage.

To this end, the Recommendation spells out the measures which should be taken whereby pre-print material or archival quality copies of moving images may be acquired by public or private non-profit-making institutions. Such measures include the institution of mandatory deposit systems for moving images of national production; the deposit of foreign productions should be the subject of voluntary arrangements. The Recommendation calls for the establishment of film and television archives where they do not exist, and invites States to provide them with appropriate resources in terms of staff, equipment and funds. The items deposited should be preserved in these establishments and processed according to the highest archival standards, since poor storage conditions accelerate the deterioration process to which the material supports are continuously subject.

While taking due account of the relevant provisions of international conventions and national legislation concerning copyright and the protection of performers, producers of phonograms and broadcasting organizations, the Recommenda-

---

1. Adopted by the Unesco General Conference at its twenty-first session, held at Belgrade, on 27 October 1980.

tion provides that officially recognized archives should be permitted, within certain limits, to utilize the deposited material. Thus such archives might be entitled to permit the viewing of a projection copy on a non-profit-making basis by a limited number of viewers for purposes of teaching, scholarship or research, provided that such use does not conflict with the normal exploitation of the work.

At the international level, States are invited to associate their efforts in order to promote the safeguarding and preservation of moving images, in particular those countries which do not possess appropriate facilities or adequate resources. The Recommendation also calls for States to co-operate for the purpose of enabling any State to gain access to moving images that relate to its history or culture and of which it does not hold either pre-print material or projection copies.

United Nations Educational, Scientific and
Cultural Organization

Recommendation for the Safeguarding and Preservation of Moving Images

Adopted by the General Conference at its
twenty-first session, Belgrade, 27 October 1980

The General Conference of the United Nations Educational, Scientific and Cultural Organization, meeting in Belgrade from 23 September to 28 October 1980, at its twenty-first session,

Considering that moving images are an expression of the cultural identity of peoples, and because of their educational, cultural, artistic, scientific and historical value, form an integral part of a nation's cultural heritage,

Considering that moving images constitute new forms of expression, particularly characteristic of present-day society, whereby an important and ever-increasing part of contemporary culture is manifested,

Considering that moving images also provide a fundamental means of recording the unfolding of events and, as such, constitute important and often unique testimonies, of a new dimension, to the history, way of life and culture of peoples and to the evolution of the universe,

Noting that moving images have an increasingly important role to play as a means of communication and mutual understanding among all the peoples of the world,

Noting furthermore that, by disseminating knowledge and culture throughout the world, moving images contribute extensively to the education and to the enrichment of each human being,

Considering however that, due to the nature of their material embodiment and the various methods of their fixation, moving images are extremely vulnerable and should be maintained under specific technical conditions,

Noting furthermore that many elements of the moving image heritage have disappeared due to deterioration, accident or unwarranted disposal, which constitutes an irreversible impoverishment of that heritage,

Recognizing the results yielded by the efforts of specialized institutions to save moving images from the dangers to which they are exposed,

Considering that it is necessary for each State to take the appropriate complementary measures to ensure the safeguarding and preservation for posterity of this particularly fragile part of its cultural heritage, just as other forms of cultural property are safeguarded and preserved as a source of enrichment for present and future generations,

Considering at the same time that the appropriate measures to ensure the safeguarding and preservation of moving images should be taken with due regard for freedom of opinion, expression and information, recognized as an essential part of human rights and fundamental freedoms inherent in the dignity of the human being, for the need to strengthen peace and international understanding and for the legitimate position of copyright holders and of all the holders of other rights in moving images,

Recognizing also the rights of States to take appropriate measures for the safeguarding and preservation of moving images, taking into account their obligations under international law,

Considering that moving images created by the peoples of the world also form part of the heritage of mankind as a whole and consequently that closer international co-operation should be promoted to safeguard and preserve these irreplaceable records of human activity and, in particular, for the benefit of those countries with limited resources,

Considering furthermore that, due to increasing international co-operation, imported moving images have an important role in the cultural life of most countries,

Considering that important aspects of the history and culture of certain countries, and, in particular, of those previously colonized, are recorded in the form of moving images which are not always accessible to the countries concerned,

Noting that the General Conference has already adopted international instruments relating to the protection of the movable cultural heritage and, in particular, the Convention for the Protection of Cultural Property in the Event of Armed Conflict (1954), the Recommendation on the Means of Prohibiting and Preventing the Illicit Export, Import and Transfer of Ownership of Cultural Property (1964), the Convention on the Means of Prohibiting and Preventing the Illicit Import, Export and Transfer of Ownership of Cultural Property (1970), the Recommendation on the International Exchange of Cultural Property (1976), the Recommendation on the Protection of Movable Cultural Property (1978),

Desiring to supplement and extend the application of the standards and principles laid down in these conventions and recommendations,

Bearing in mind the terms of the Universal Copyright Convention, the Berne Convention for the Protection of Literary and Artistic Works and the Convention for the Protection of Performers, Producers of Phonograms and Broadcasting Organizations,

Having before it proposals concerning the safeguarding and preservation of moving images,

Having decided, at its twentieth session, that this question should be the subject of a Recommendation to Member States,

Adopts, this twenty-seventh day of October 1980, the present Recommendation:

The General Conference recommends that Member States apply the following provisions by taking whatever legislative or other steps may be required, in conformity with the constitutional system or practice of each State, to give effect within their respective territories to the principles and norms formulated in this Recommendation.

The General Conference recommends that Member States bring this Recommendation to the attention of the appropriate authorities and bodies.

The General Conference recommends that Member States submit to it, by the dates and in the form which it shall prescribe, reports concerning the action taken by them in pursuance of this Recommendation.

I. Definitions

1. For the purposes of this Recommendation:
(a) 'moving images' shall be taken to mean any series of images recorded on a support (irrespective of the method of recording or of the nature of the support, such as film, tape or disc, used in their initial or subsequent fixation), with or without accompanying sound, which when projected impart an impression of motion and which are intended for communication or distribution to the public or are made for documentation purposes; they shall be taken to include *inter alia* items in the following categories:
    (i) cinematographic productions (such as feature films, short films, popular science films, newsreels and documentaries, animated and educational films);
    (ii) television productions made by or for broadcasting organizations;
    (iii) videographic productions (contained in videograms) other than those referred to under (i) and (ii) above;
(b) 'pre-print material' shall be taken to mean the material support for moving images, consisting in the case of a cinematographic film of a negative,

internegative or interpositive, and in the case of a videogram of a master, such pre-print material being intended for the procurement of copies;

(c) 'projection copy' shall be taken to mean the material support for moving images intended for actual viewing and/or the communication of the images.

2. For the purposes of this Recommendation, 'national production' shall be taken to mean moving images, the maker or at least one of the co-makers of which has his headquarters or habitual residence within the territory of the State concerned.

II. General principles

3. All moving images of national production should be considered by Member States as an integral part of their 'moving image heritage'. Moving images of original foreign production may also form part of the cultural heritage of a country when they are of particular national importance from the point of view of the culture or history of the country concerned. Should it not be possible for his heritage to be handed down in its entirety to future generations for technical or financial reasons, as large a proportion as possible should be safeguarded and preserved. The necessary arrangements should be made to ensure that concerted action is taken by all the public and private bodies concerned in order to elaborate and apply an active policy to this end.

4. The appropriate measures should be taken to ensure that the moving image heritage is afforded adequate physical protection from the depredations wrought by time and by the environment. Since poor storage conditions accelerate the deterioration process to which the material supports are continuously subject and may even lead to their total destruction, moving images should be preserved in officially recognized film and television archives and processed according to the highest archival standards. Furthermore, research should be specifically directed towards the development of high quality and lasting support-media for the proper safeguarding and preservation of moving images.

5. Measures should be taken to prevent the loss, unwarranted disposal or deterioration of any item of the national production. Means should therefore be instituted in each country whereby pre-print material or archival quality copies of moving images may be systematically acquired, safeguarded and preserved in public or private non-profit-making archival institutions.

6. Access should be made available as far as possible to the works and information sources represented by moving images which are acquired, safeguarded and preserved by public and private non-profit-making institutions. Their utilization should not prejudice either the legitimate rights or the interests of those involved in the making and exploitation thereof, in accordance with the provisions of the Universal Copyright Convention, the Berne Convention for the Protection of Literary and Artistic Works and the Convention for the Protection of Performers, Producers of Phonograms and Broadcasting Organizations, and national legislation.

7. In order to ensure that a truly effective safeguarding and preservation programme is successfully undertaken, the co-operation of all those involved in the making, distribution, safeguarding and preservation of moving images should be obtained. Public information activities should therefore be organized in particular with a view to instilling in the professional circles concerned a general awareness of the significance of moving images for a country's heritage and the consequent need to safeguard and preserve them as testimonies to the life of contemporary society.

III. Measures recommended

8. In accordance with the principles set out above, and in conformity with their normal constitutional practice, Member States are invited to take all the necessary steps, including the provision to officially recognized archives of appropriate resources in terms of staff, equipment and funds, to safeguard and preserve effectively their moving image heritage in accordance with the following guidelines:

Legal and administrative measures

9. To ensure that moving images forming part of the cultural heritage of countries are systematically preserved, Member States are invited to take measures whereby officially recognized archives are able to acquire for safeguarding and preservation any part or all of their country's national production. Such measures may include, for example, voluntary arrangements with the holders of rights for the deposit of moving images, acquisition of moving images by purchase or donation or the institution of mandatory deposit systems through appropriate legislation or administrative measures. Such systems should complement and coexist with existing archival arrangements relating to publicly owned moving images. Measures taken should be consistent with the provisions of national legislation and international instruments concerning the protection of human rights, copyright and the protection of performers, pro-

ducers of phonograms and broadcasting organizations relating to moving images, and should take into account the special conditions provided in favour of developing countries in certain of these instruments. When mandatory deposit systems are adopted, they should provide that:

(a) moving images of national production, whatever the physical characteristics of their support medium or the purpose for which they were created, should be deposited in at least one complete copy of the highest archival quality, preferably in the form of pre-print material;

(b) the material should be deposited by the maker—as defined by national legislation—having his headquarters or habitual residence within the territory of the State concerned, irrespective of any co-production arrangement made with a foreign maker;

(c) the material deposited should be preserved in officially recognized film or television archives; where they do not exist, every effort should be made to establish such institutions at the national and/or regional level; pending the establishment of officially recognized archives, the material should be provisionally stored in appropriately equipped premises;

(d) the deposit should be made as soon as possible within a maximum time-limit fixed by national regulations;

(e) the depositor should have controlled access to the deposited material whenever further printing is required, on condition that such access does not cause any damage to or deterioration of the material deposited;

(f) the officially recognized archives should be entitled, subject to the relevant provisions of international conventions and of national legislation governing copyright and the protection of performers, producers of phonograms and broadcasting organizations, to:

   (i) take all the necessary measures in order to safeguard and preserve the moving image heritage, and, where possible, to enhance the technical quality; where the reproduction of moving images is involved, due regard should be given to all the rights in the images concerned;

   (ii) permit the viewing on their premises of a projection copy on a non-profit-making basis by a limited number of viewers for purposes of teaching, scholarship or research, provided that such use does not conflict with the normal exploitation of the work and on condition that no deterioration of or damage to the material deposited is thereby caused;

(g) the material deposited and the copies made therefrom should not be used for any other purposes, nor should their contents be modified;

(h) officially recognized archives should be entitled to request users to make a reasonable contribution to the cost of the services provided.

10.   The safeguarding and preservation of all moving images of national production should be regarded as the highest objective. However, until such time as developments in technology make this feasible everywhere, in those cases where it is not possible, for technical reasons of cost or space, to record all publicly broadcast moving images or to safeguard and preserve on a long-term basis all the material deposited, each Member State is invited to establish the principles for determining which images should be recorded and/or deposited for posterity, including 'ephemeral recordings' having an exceptional documentary character. Those moving images which, because of their educational, cultural, artistic, scientific and historical value, form part of a nation's cultural heritage should be retained on a priority basis. Any system introduced to this end should foresee that selection should be based on the broadest possible consensus of informed opinion and should take particular account of the appraisal criteria established by the archival profession. Furthermore, due care should be taken to prevent the elimination of material until sufficient time has elapsed to allow for the necessary perspective. Material eliminated in this way should be returned to the depositor.

11.   Foreign producers, and those responsible for the public distribution of moving images made abroad, should be encouraged, in accordance with the spirit of this Recommendation and without prejudice to the free movement of moving images across national borders, to deposit voluntarily in the officially recognized archives of the countries in which they are publicly distributed a copy of moving images of the highest archival quality, subject to all the rights therein. In particular, those responsible for the distribution of moving images, dubbed or subtitled in the language or languages of the country in which they are publicly distributed, which are regarded as an integral part of the moving image heritage of the country concerned or which are of significant value for the cultural needs of teaching or research, should be urged to deposit the material relating to these images in the spirit of international co-operation. Officially recognized archives should seek establishment of such deposit systems and, furthermore, the acquisition, subject to all the rights therein, of copies of moving images which are of exceptional universal value, even if they have not been publicly distributed in the country concerned. Control of and access to such material should be governed by the provisions of paragraph 9(e), (f), (g) and (h) above.

12.   Member States are invited to conduct follow-up studies on the effectiveness of the measures proposed in paragraph 11. If, following a reasonable trial period, the suggested form of voluntary deposit fails to ensure the adequate safeguarding and preservation of adapted moving images that are of particular national importance from the standpoint of the culture or history of a State,

it would be for the State concerned, under the provisions of its national legislation, to define such measures as would prevent the disappearance, particularly through destruction, of copies of adapted moving images, due regard being given to the rights of all those holding legitimate rights in such moving images of particular national importance.

13. Member States are invited furthermore to investigate the feasibility of permitting—taking due account of international conventions concerning copyright and the protection of performers, producers of phonograms and broadcasting organizations—officially recognized archives to utilize the deposited material for research and recognized teaching purposes provided that such utilization does not conflict with the normal exploitation of the works.

Technical measures

14. Member States are invited to pay due attention to the archival standards concerning storage and treatment of moving images recommended by the international organizations competent in the field of the safeguarding and preservation of moving images.

15. Furthermore, Member States are invited to make the necessary arrangements to ensure that the institutions responsible for safeguarding and preserving the moving image heritage take the following measures:
(a) establish and make available national filmographies and catalogues of all categories of moving images and descriptions of their holdings, seeking, where possible, the standardization of cataloguing systems; these documentary materials would together form an inventory of the country's moving image heritage;
(b) collect, preserve and make available for research purposes institutional records, personal papers and other material that document the origin, production, distribution and projection of moving images, subject to the agreement of those concerned;
(c) maintain in good condition the equipment, some of which may no longer be in general use but which may be necessary for the reproduction and projection of material preserved or, should that not prove possible, ensure that the moving images concerned are transferred onto another material support permitting their reproduction and projection;
(d) ensure that the standards applicable to the storage, safeguarding, preservation, restoration and duplication of moving images are rigorously applied;
(e) as far as possible, improve the technical quality of the moving images to be safeguarded and preserved, ensuring that they are in a condition con-

ducive to their long-term and effective storage and use; when treatment involves the reproduction of material, due regard should be given to all the rights in the images concerned.

16. Member States are invited to encourage private bodies and individuals holding moving images to take the necessary steps to ensure the safeguarding and preservation of these images under adequate technical conditions. These bodies and individuals should be encouraged to entrust to officially recognized archives the pre-print material if available or, in default thereof, copies of moving images made before the introduction of the deposit system.

Supplementary measures

17. Member States are invited to encourage the competent authorities and other bodies concerned with the safeguarding and preservation of moving images to undertake public information activities in order to:
(a) promote among all those involved in the making and distribution of moving images an appreciation of the lasting value of such images from the educational, cultural, artistic, scientific and historical points of view and an awareness of the consequent need to collaborate in their safeguarding and preservation;
(b) draw the attention of the public at large to the educational, cultural, artistic, scientific and historical importance of moving images and to the measures necessary for their safeguarding and preservation.

18. Measures should be taken at the national level in order to co-ordinate research in fields related to the safeguarding and preservation of moving images and to encourage research specifically directed towards their long-term preservation at a reasonable cost. Information on methods and techniques for safeguarding and preserving moving images, including the results of relevant research, should be disseminated to all concerned.

19. Training programmes in the safeguarding and restoration of moving images should be organized, covering the most recent methods and techniques.

IV. International co-operation

20. Member States are invited to associate their efforts in order to promote the safeguarding and preservation of moving images which form part of the cultural heritage of nations. Such co-operation should be stimulated by the

IV.B.12

competent international governmental and non-governmental organizations and should comprise the following measures:

(a) participation in international programmes for the establishment of the necessary infrastructure at the regional or national level, to safeguard and preserve the moving image heritage of countries which do not possess appropriate facilities or adequate resources;

(b) exchange of information on methods and techniques for the safeguarding and preservation of moving images and, in particular, on the findings of recent research;

(c) organization of national or international training courses in related fields in particular for nationals of developing countries;

(d) joint action for the standardization of cataloguing methods specifically intended for archival holdings of moving images;

(e) authorization, subject to the relevant provisions of international conventions and of national legislation governing copyright and the protection of performers, producers of phonograms and broadcasting organizations, of the lending of copies of moving images to other officially recognized archives exclusively for purposes of teaching, scholarship or research, provided that the consent of the holders of rights and the archives concerned is obtained to such lending and that no deterioration of or damage to the material lent is thereby caused.

21. Technical co-operation should be provided in particular to developing countries, in order to ensure or facilitate the adequate safeguarding and preservation of their moving image heritage.

22. Member States are invited to co-operate for the purpose of enabling any State to gain access to moving images that relate to its history or culture and of which it does not hold either pre-print material or projection copies. To this end each Member State is invited:

(a) to facilitate, in the case of moving images on deposit in officially recognized archives and which relate to the history or culture of another country, the acquisition by the officially recognized archives of that country of either pre-print material or a projection copy thereof;

(b) to encourage private bodies or institutions within its territory which hold such moving images to deposit on a voluntary basis either pre-print material or a projection copy thereof with the officially recognized archives of the country concerned.

Where necessary, the material supplied in accordance with (a) and (b) above should be made available against reimbursement of the cost by the requesting body. However, in view of the cost involved, pre-print material or projection copies of moving images held by Member States as public property and which relate to the history and culture of developing countries be made available to the officially recognized archives of those countries under especially favourable conditions. Any material provided in accordance with this paragraph should be made available subject to any copyright and any rights of performers, producers of phonograms or broadcasting organizations which may exist therein.

23.   When moving images forming part of a country's cultural or historical heritage have been lost by that country, whatever the circumstances, and in particular as a consequence of colonial or foreign occupation, Member States are invited, in connection with request for such images, to co-operate in the spririt of resolution 5/10.1/1, III, adopted by the General Conference as its twentieth session.

IV.B.12